MAXIMIZE YOUR INFLUENCE

HOW TO MAKE DIGITAL MEDIA WORK FOR YOUR CHURCH, YOUR MINISTRY, AND YOU

PHIL COOKE

Published via the combined efforts of:

Cooke Media Group
Burbank, CA 91505
info@cookemediagroup.com
www.cookemediagroup.com
818-303-2424

Insight International, Inc.
Tulsa, OK 74137
contact@freshword.com
www.freshword.com
918-493-1718

ISBN: 978-1-943361-69-4
E-book ISBN: 978-1-943361-70-0

Library of Congress Control Number: 2020910769

Printed in the United States of America.

ENDORSEMENTS

"Phil is an expert in the field of digital media with a passion for helping pastors and ministry leaders worldwide. He is uniquely gifted to teach leaders a digital worldview that honors God and connects with people where they are. His book is an incredible resource for leaders to gain practical tips, as well as high level concepts, on how to utilize creative teams to get results and feel comfortable engaging in digital conversations. Read this book and learn from one of the best voices in the field of digital media!"

–Bobby Gruenewald
Pastor of Innovation at Life.Church
Founder of the YouVersion Bible App

"If there ever was a manual for helping Christian leaders navigate the media . . . this is it! Phil Cooke's passion for the Church and its responsibility through media is unparalleled. This timely book will challenge your thinking while offering tried and tested solutions from Phil's longevity in the media landscape."

–Ben Field
Head of Film and Television at Hillsong Church

"I am struck with Phil's passion to empower pastors and ministry leaders with easy-to-navigate insights and accessible tools—essential to lead others well in today's digital era. His big-picture approach gifts us with an eagle's eye view to easily understand the cultural and digital landscape laid before us. While apps and media-informed platforms constantly change, digital engagement is here to stay. And, if we embrace the attainable concepts presented here, surely the world will see the glory of God—in creative, life-changing ways—as the message meets them exactly where they are!"

–Dr. Rob Hoskins
President and CEO of OneHope

"For over fifteen years, I have been recommending my friend Phil Cooke to anyone wanting to maximize their influence. I love what he's been doing for decades. I love even more who he is—his heart; and how he thinks. His vast historical experience has not kept him from being an explorer continuously searching the horizons. In *Maximize Your Influence*, Phil Cooke will take you thirty thousand feet in the air and let you see possibilities, both present and future, for you to accomplish your dreams, personally and professionally. Read yourself and get a copy for all you lead."

–Sam Chand
Leadership Consultant
Author of *Leadership Pain*
www.samchand.com

CONTENTS

ACKNOWLEDGEMENTS

Writing this book has only been possible because of a great core team at our production and consulting company, Cooke Media Group. While I was hunkered down in writing mode, Dan Wathen was managing a long slate of media projects around the world, Dawn Nicole Baldwin was developing and executing amazing client strategies, Chris Guerra was keeping our online presence humming, and Victoria Hansen was hosting Zoom calls, juggling communication, and managing travel schedules for the team.

Aside from her regular writing and producing responsibilities, Laura Woodworth stepped in and edited this manuscript and was quick to tell me what worked and what didn't. I've often said that I'm not a *writer*, I'm a *rewriter*. Novelist John Irving said it better: "Half my life is an act of revision." So thanks Laura for making me rethink everything.

Most of all, I need to thank my wife Kathleen, who knew me before I learned much about film, video, or anything else related to media. She cofounded our production and consulting company, and in the process, we've walked this road together, learned it together, and lived it together. And who knew it would all begin in college when she accepted a date over the phone with a guy she thought was someone else.

It was the start of the greatest adventure of my life.

INTRODUCTION

"Ministry is tough. It's not for the faint of heart."
—K. Marshall Williams

This book is written for pastors and ministry leaders. I've spent my entire life behind the scenes at churches, ministries, and nonprofits, and know a little about what those men and women face. My father was a pastor in Charlotte, North Carolina, and it would be tough to guess how many communion cups I've filled, how many bulletins I've duplicated (remember "mimeograph" machines?), and how many times I mowed the church cemetery. In between those jobs, I watched my father spend hours prepping sermons, comforting families at funeral homes, fixing the plumbing, and doing anything else that needed attention. My mom received very little credit, but if it wasn't for her, we wouldn't have had a children's program, the church bulletins would have never been written, the ladies never mobilized, church suppers and events never organized, my dad supported, and there would have been no one to take me to track meets or Boy Scouts.

> For all of its challenges, growing up with that
> small church congregation probably taught me
> more about juggling multiple tasks and learning
> people skills than anything else I've ever done.

Since that time, I've spent decades working with pastors and ministry leaders of all kinds, helping them share their message and calling through media. As a result, I've learned even more about how they think, and the unique challenges they face living in today's media-driven culture—a distracted, cluttered culture my father never had to deal with in his day. Plus, I know from experience that while Christian universities, Bible colleges, and seminaries generally do an excellent job of training students to preach, counsel, and understand the Bible, they do a pretty poor job of teaching those students how to use social media, websites, short videos, and other digital tools to connect with their community, amplify their message, or promote their church or ministry.

That's where I come in.

This book isn't a detailed, technical look at social media platforms, websites, YouTube channels, broadcasting, publishing, and other areas. It won't teach you how to build a website or create a social media strategy. It's an *overview* that will help you speak the language of web designers, video producers, publishers, and marketers. It will teach you about book agents, media buyers, and how to inspire volunteers. It's not for your team as much as it is for *you*. It will help you understand enough about each discipline and platform to feel comfortable in the digital conversation, so that crazy idea you see in your head can actually be expressed to your team.

As a leader, you don't have to understand the complexities of your website's user experience, but you should know a little about what it is and why it matters. Even after the COVID-19 church lockdown, I still meet pastors (and some elder boards) who are terrified of live streaming their services because they believe church attendance will drop (I'll deal with that fear later), and I've met a horrifying number of leaders who have no clue about how to maximize the creative team around them.

This is your ticket to understanding the digital revolution and making it work for you.

This is also a very personal perspective. This is my advice, written as if I was personally coaching you and your church or ministry, which is why it's about the *concepts*, not the *details*. In other words, whether you lead a congregation of twenty or lead a church of twenty thousand this information will help take your ministry to the next level. After all, technology changes, and many of the platforms, apps, and some techniques I mention in the book may be changed or even gone by the time you read this. Likewise, how people *consume* media is constantly changing. Your team can keep up with the detailed changes, but as long as you understand the *principles and purpose* of sharing your story through the media, you can easily weather changes in the tools and platforms.

One of the most frustrating issues I see out there among churches and ministries is leaders who are afraid to explore these communication platforms because they simply don't understand how they work. And when we don't understand something, we often hesitate because we worry we'll look stupid in front of the congregation or team.

That is a big reason for this book.

One of my great purposes in life is to help ministry leaders understand how to communicate in today's digital world well enough to be *confident.* Insecure leaders rarely take risks, even when those risks could have enormous benefits. And in my opinion, rarely has there been a more important time in history to take risks for the sake of the gospel.

In our book, *The Way Back: How Christians Blew Our Credibility and How We Get It Back,* cowriter Jonathan Bock and I present the case that the reason Christianity is disappearing from our culture isn't because of bad marketing or branding (although we could do better there), but we simply aren't living the life God has called us to live. We don't have a "marketing" problem; we have a "salesforce" problem. Christians today simply don't believe in the product.

But I also strongly believe that one of the challenges we face is that *we don't communicate the story of the gospel well in today's digital culture.* Other belief systems, lifestyles, organizations, movements, and cults are growing because they have mastered communicating in a digital age, but churches generally lag far behind—to a great degree because the leader lags behind.

"The speed of the boss is the speed of the team."
—Automotive Executive Lee Iacocca

Think about it—as I write this, according to a National Congregations Study, there are roughly 384,000 churches in the United States alone, which means that all the other religions, causes, and advocacy groups combined don't even come close to that number. It's like being part of a global organization with multiple local offices in nearly every town and city in the world. And yet, many of those other (and much smaller) organizations are growing exponentially, while the influence of Christianity continues to shrink. A significant reason most of those other organizations are experiencing explosive growth is they simply have mastered the art of telling their story through media. They are part of a contemporary cultural conversation that has left much of the Church behind.

But what if the majority of pastors and leaders of our 384,000 churches could learn how to speak that language? What if every church in America had a voice sharing the gospel to their communities via social media, short videos, websites, television, and publishing? What if they understood the demographic changes so well, they could immediately adapt their message to a shifting culture?

The question is—*What if they cared enough about reaching people in their communities that they were willing to learn? And for those who already know that language, were willing to improve?*

Hopefully, this book will help both groups of leaders.

WHY ME?

When I started working in media, a single video camera cost more than $250,000, and was so big that without a sturdy truck and large crew, it was impossible to take it on location. At the time, I was a student working part time on a crew producing prime time television specials for the most watched religious TV program in America. In those days there were only three TV channels, and the audience—even for religious programming—was massive.

After graduating from college I went to Hollywood for a year, but I was eventually drawn back into the world of "Christian" television. (As a disclaimer, I must admit that I was getting married and needed a steady job.) Since then, I've had forays into major secular advertising and commercial production, film projects, and other media opportunities, but my heart has always been focused on helping Christians engage today's culture more effectively through media.

That means during my career, I've been involved at some level in the growth of every media platform that has been used or is still being used to share the message of the gospel. In those early days a national media ministry was funded through direct mail, but today, we're seeing a significant part of that giving transition online. As video equipment became more affordable, we've seen a shift from major media ministries to local churches catching a vision for using television to reach their communities. In fact, quite a number of churches have actually produced feature motion pictures.

The advent of short video and live streaming expanded that trend even more. And social media? Let's just say that it should be a vital part of any church or ministry's strategy for reaching their community and beyond.

> **With a Ph.D. in theology mixed with decades spent in media production, I have a unique take on media opportunities available to pastors and other Christian leaders.**

Over that time our team at Cooke Media Group has worked with many of the largest and most effective churches and ministries around the world. I've produced programming or taught media in nearly one hundred countries, and discovered just how hungry church leaders outside the United States are for this information.

While technical details are important, my focus is more on the "big picture." What are we doing right and what are we doing wrong? Why is Christian influence disappearing as the influence of media grows? What are we missing by not engaging this generation more effectively? What media platforms and strategies are really working?

We have more opportunities to share our message with more people than any time in the history of the world.

I'll talk a bit later about how an unknown monk named Martin Luther leveraged the new world of publishing to become the most influential writer and preacher of his age. Leaders like Billy Graham, Oral Roberts, and Fulton Sheen were pioneers in sharing the gospel on prime time television.

But today, with digital publishing, a video camera in our pocket, social media, and much more, we have more tools at our fingertips than leaders just a generation ago could have imagined. Keep in mind that there are now film festivals for movies shot on mobile phones, so don't even try telling me all the reasons you can't get your message to a larger audience.

You may be leading a small church or ministry and only have one person you can trust with communication or media issues. Fine. Start there. But as you grow, I would encourage you to put more effort into developing your creative team because that is a launching pad for growth.

We'll talk more about that later. But for now, I can tell you this: in my experience, at most of the high impact churches and ministries in this country, after the pastor or leader, the communication director or creative director is the most influential voice in the organization. That's because those leaders know that communication and media are the keys to amplifying their message to millions of people beyond their walls.

The building program matters. Church education matters.
The missions' budget matters. But it's time to
put communication and media on the priority list.

And speaking of missions, one of the greatest gifts a local church can give their missionaries in other countries is helping them with media. My wife Kathleen and I launched a ministry organization called The Influence Lab for the express purpose of teaching and training the global Church to use media more effectively. At any given moment, I have multiple requests on my desk from churches, ministry organizations, and leaders outside the United States asking us to come and train their communication and media teams.

So yes, this knowledge will help your message transcend the walls of your local church, but it will also take your message to a world in need. In fact, that global need is so great that it's time to stop thinking of "missions" just in terms of *geographic* boundaries. We need to start thinking of missions in terms of *digital* boundaries as well.

The power of media is far greater than we can imagine.

One thing to note: This is not a normal book designed to be read straight through. Feel free to skip around and go right to the areas where you need help the most or feel particularly called. If you're already a force to be reckoned with on social media, perhaps you should check out the section on book publishing, or how short videos can help tell your story. If fundraising is your weak point, by all means start there.

Many of the sections have been taken from my blog at PhilCooke.com where I write about the intersection of faith, media, and culture. As a result, it's designed around short sections and thoughts that are quick to read and easy to digest.

You'll also notice that it's filled with checklists. I'm partial to lists because they are direct and to the point. I've written it that way to help you get right to the heart of the issues, as well as use this material to teach your team more easily.

As such, this is a book designed to stay on or near your desk as a reference. It will help you speak the language of creativity, help express your ideas to your communication team if you have one, and help you do it yourself if you don't. Mostly, my goal is to challenge you to keep up. The world has changed and will continue changing, whether we like it or not and whether we're ready or not.

So let's get going . . .

— 1 —

DIGITAL THINKING

"The digital revolution is far more significant than the invention of writing or even of printing."
—Douglas Engelbart

In 2020, when the COVID-19 virus caused churches to be temporarily closed and people were sent home, we experienced a dramatic change in the way most pastors and church leaders viewed media. For many, it had been an "add-on," or something that was "nice but not necessary." A surprising number still felt that ministering to people online or through media wasn't really "ministry." In fact, Lifeway Research reported that before the crisis, 41 percent of churches had never offered any worship services or other resources online at all.

But within a week, things dramatically changed.

Most of this book was written before the crisis, but as it was about to be published, the pandemic hit, and I needed to update the manuscript. Since that time I've added more information so that it will be relevant far into the future. My hope is that for all the pastors who understand the power of media, this will be an important reference.

It's no secret that reaching a congregation, community, or media audience in today's distracted and disrupted world is a real challenge. Although we have more channels for reaching them than ever before, those very channels slice up the audience, making it more difficult than ever to actually connect. As a result, when leaders engage our team at Cooke Media Group to help them share their story, we walk them through a process we customize with every leader to clarify and focus their message, find the right audience, then explore the tools to maximize the sharing of that message.

Without giving away our "secret sauce," here's a handful of the issues we explore with our clients, and why this book is so important. As you read them, consider how they could impact your own message or story:

It all starts with strategy, which is the art of discovering what sets you apart and who would care most about your message, cause, or story. Today it takes more than someone with a video camera, a social media director, or a graphic designer to communicate your message. Before any of those team members start working, it's critical to find the answer to "why," and that is a leader's job.

It's been said that any soldier can take the hill, but a leader knows which hill to take and why it needs to be taken in the first place. Far too many churches allow the big picture decision making to be made by other members of the staff. In a large church or ministry with an experienced, high level communication or media team, that can be a good thing, but with less experienced members it could be a disaster. And in either case, it should never happen without the input and insight from the pastor or ministry leader.

THE BIG PICTURE MATTERS

Our creative team helps churches, ministries, and nonprofit organizations create websites, launch social media campaigns, produce media programming like documentaries and TV shows, and create amazing videos. At any given time we're working with various clients on the kind of media projects that inspire and motivate their audience, congregation, or donors. And over the years, we've learned a key principle that helps our clients again and again: *Be focused on the bigger picture.*

Whatever you do in media—build a website, produce a video, launch a marketing campaign, publish a book, or whatever—understand that each of those elements are part of a much bigger story and strategy. In today's distracted world, where people are being overwhelmed with communication and media messages, anything you create has to be part of a bigger, multi-platform strategy to maximize those opportunities.

Talented video, social media, and communication teams with brilliant ideas are a great start, but until they understand the bigger strategy of how to reach your audience, you'll never make an impact. It's been said that if you want to know which road to take, it helps to first know where you're going.

Think before you produce.
Ask the "why" before you explore the "how."

Then, once we define your why, we bring that to life with messaging—clarifying exactly what your message or story should be at this moment. Oddly enough, most of our clients try to communicate too much—largely because they're thinking of themselves, and not the audience they want to reach.

In a cluttered world, *simplicity* and *clarity*
are what get people's attention.

Certainly many organizations and visionary leaders have much to share, but in today's hyper-competitive world, most people respond to too much information by shutting down and turning off. So it's essential that we stream-line the message and focus on what matters from the audience's perspective.

Speaking of clutter, identity development is a key step in our process since "perception" is so important in a distracted world. We'll discuss branding and positioning in a later section, but it's important to know how sensitive perceptions are in a distracted world. Positioning is essential to help your message rise above the noise because it focuses on what your audience thinks, what they need, and how you fit into their lives. This goes beyond your brand and is often overlooked by many organizations.

Finally, deciding how to share your ministry or organization's message is vital, via social media, short video production, broadcast radio or TV, movie, live events, blogging, podcasting, live streaming and more.

It's not how you want to reach them, it's how they want to reach you.

There's no point in creating the best podcast ever produced if your audience is somewhere else. That's why finding the right platforms are so important for connecting with your audience.

These steps aren't designed to overwhelm you or make you think that engaging media is too complex or difficult. My purpose is to remind you that a high school kid with a video camera isn't enough. A talented graphic designer isn't enough. Even a well-intentioned communication director isn't enough—if you haven't spent time thinking about the bigger picture.

These days, a great number of leaders and teams recognize the power of media, but don't understand the best way to leverage that power. There was a time when sharing a message meant standing on a soapbox and talking to people passing by, preaching in a pulpit, or printing a book or newspaper. But today with an almost endless number of media options, making the right decision about the what, when, where, how, and why of your message can be the difference between success and failure.

The stakes are high, and your message matters. Choose carefully.

EVERYTHING COMMUNICATES

Another issue leaders, speakers, and communicators often fail to understand is that in today's digital world, *everything communicates*. That means it's not just the message you share, but it's the clothes you're wearing, your attitude, the way you stand, the lighting in the room, the social media platform you use, and many more things that impact how people receive that message.

Whether you wear a coat and tie or skinny jeans impact how people receive your message. It's the same whether you present alone or with a PowerPoint presentation. I could name multiple factors that can impact your message in a meeting, from the pulpit, in a video, or online, but you get the idea.

Studies have shown that because we're so distracted and pulled in so many different directions, that when we meet someone for the first time, we decide what we think of that person within the first eight seconds. Think about that for a minute. You haven't really heard what they have to say, and you don't really know them very well at all, but in today's hyper-competitive, distracted, digital world, we've changed our behavior so that we're making decisions about things we don't even yet understand.

Which is the reason I tell pastors that I'm thrilled that your sermon is anointed and your worship is powerful, but in an eight second world, what's the parking experience like? What's the church lobby look like? Who's the first person a new visitor meets when they walk in the door? Today, new visitors are making decisions about your church long before they actually reach the pew.

In the same way, I've also discovered that virtually 100 percent of potential new visitors will check out the church online before they visit. So why are many church websites so lame?

Even when you're not communicating, *that* communicates a message.

Whether you're preaching a sermon, developing a business proposal, speaking at a conference, hosting a video, recording a podcast, or talking to your best friend, there's a wealth of information that gets communicated *beyond* the essential message.

COMMUNICATION IS A TWO-WAY CONVERSATION

That's why generation after generation pastors and Christian leaders get it wrong. They believe our only responsibility is sharing the message. But we also have a responsibility to do our best to make sure that message is received. To be honest, this new two-way conversation is remarkably similar to the method of worship during the days of the early Church. Frank Viola and George Barna, writing in their book, *Pagan Christianity: Exploring the Roots of Our Church Practices,* reveal some of the most common practices of worship in the early Church, including:

-> *Active participation and interruptions by the audience were common.*

-> *Prophets and priests spoke extemporaneously and out of a present burden, rather than from a set script.*

-> *There is no indication that Old Testament prophets or priests gave regular speeches to God's people. Instead, the nature of Old Testament preaching was sporadic, fluid, and open for audience participation. Preaching in the ancient synagogue followed a similar pattern.*

Wayne E. Oates, writing in *Pastoral Counseling,* put it this way: "The original proclamation of the Christian message was a two-way conversation . . . but when the oratorical schools of the Western world laid hold of the Christian message, they made Christian preaching something vastly different. Oratory tended to take the place of conversation. The greatness of the orator took the place of the astounding event of Jesus Christ. And the dialogue between speaker and listener faded into a monologue."

That's not to say that preaching or proclaiming the gospel isn't important, but it does indicate that today's technology is actually giving us the capability to recover many of the styles and ideals of the early Church. The two-way conversation that began in Jerusalem became a one-way conversation with the influence of Greco-Roman culture; and now in the digital age, we are once again rediscovering the power of *dialogue over monologue.*

In the open world of the future, those who simply preach or teach without regard to the way the audience understands and responds may simply be ignored.

THE PROPHETIC VERSUS THE PRACTICAL: SHOULD WE COMMUNICATE WHAT PEOPLE WANT OR WHAT THEY NEED?

The debate about preaching a message of "what people want" versus "what they need" isn't new. It's been debated for generations. But the issue takes on an entirely new dimension now as mass media can distribute that message to so many more people. Particularly in the digital age, wrong or destructive teaching can have enormous consequences. As a media consultant challenged with getting a message heard by the most people, I want to make that message easy to understand and easy to like. On the other hand, as a Christian sharing a prophetic message, I need to deliver a message that may cause some pain and may not be easily accepted.

Note that I use the word "prophetic" not in the sense of a direct message from God, but in the sense of "truth telling" or delivering an often difficult message based on eternal principles from scripture. As believers in Jesus Christ, our task is sharing a message that is often difficult to receive. And yet when you look at many of the top churches and religious organizations today, the messages are easy to take, inspirational, and often shallow. That's not to say a significant message of the Church shouldn't be "hope"—particularly in the nihilistic culture of death we live in today.

But I'm reminded of Dorothy Sayers (1893-1957), one of the famous "Inklings"—the group of writers at Oxford that included C. S. Lewis and J. R. R. Tolkien. In her book, *Letters to the Diminished Church,* she writes:

First, I believe it to be a grave mistake to present Christianity as something charming with no offense to it. Seeing that Christ went about the world giving the most violent offense to all kinds of people, it would seem absurd to expect that the doctrine of His person can be so presented as to offend nobody. We cannot blink at the fact that gentle Jesus, meek and mild, was so stiff in His opinions and so inflammatory in His language that He was thrown out of church, stoned, hunted from place to place, and finally gibbeted as a firebrand and a public danger.

In our present day efforts to gain an audience or write a best-selling book, I wonder if we've taken some of the distinctiveness out of our faith.

Granted, most of the people Jesus offended were the religious folks. When Jesus was confronted by sinners or the suffering, He was far more tender and gracious. He saved His most fiery volleys for the hypocritical types within the religious community.

Also, understand that when I talk about offending, I don't mean for stupid reasons. Focusing on money, Jesus junk product offers, cheesy or out of date approaches and gimmicks, or humiliating an opponent—no one has the right to be stupid in their presentation of the Christian faith.

What I'm talking about here is presenting the honest reality of the Christian faith. But today, we hear pastors try everything in their arsenal to defend a point of doctrine without actually using the scriptures. We think the audience will "relate" to it better, when it may actually be positioning the Christian faith as just another "lifestyle choice," and not the raging fire that transformed the Western world.

Are we preaching a message based on the Bible's intentions or the audience's aspirations?

Presenting the Christian faith in the media—or anywhere else for that matter—is a revolutionary act. In the 21st century, we've lulled ourselves into thinking we have to play nice to get the audience's attention when the exact opposite is true.

In my book *The Last TV Evangelist* I take on this subject directly and at length. Successful media programming in the *secular* world revolves around conflict, so why are we so afraid to speak hard truths in the Church?

WELCOME TO THE CHRISTIAN ATTACK CULTURE

Before we leave this opening section, I should mention that there's no question that the Internet has brought Christianity many wonderful things. Today we have online education available to virtually everyone, social media that encourages people to support great causes, and online communication tools that allow us to connect from the four corners of the earth. But it's also created something I believe is tearing at the very fabric of our faith.

It's created a culture of attack.

Rarely does a day go by that Christian news sites, social media streams, and other web platforms feature some Christian "correcting" another Christian—and calling them out by name. It can range from arguments over worship music, to theological squabbles, to disagreements over ministry styles, to charges of outright heresy—and the barrage of criticism has grown exponentially. While there are qualified theologians, pastors, and other leaders we should respect and listen to, there's also a tsunami of armchair theologians, angry ex-church members, and wannabes who are convinced their criticism du jour needs to be shared.

Aside from feeling comfortable "correcting" a brother or sister publicly when we've never met the person or know little about the background of what we're criticizing, a significant culprit is technology itself. With 24/7 news, and a constant barrage of blogs and social media, the Internet is bombarding us with information overload, and what may be worse—the ease of responding. As soon as we read something we don't like, all it takes is a click to send an angry reply, post a heated comment, or write an op-ed piece. I'm as guilty as anyone, and it's taken me a long time to learn to not react immediately just because I can.

The Internet has given us the illusion of intimacy. We read someone's books, articles and sermons, or watch their videos online, and we feel we know them, so why not share what we think is wrong? But that illusion of intimacy is just that—an illusion. It distracts us from the important principle of reaching out to them personally first, and making the often difficult effort of keeping it private and saving the relationship.

But then again, it's just so easy to rip them online in front of everyone and be done with it.

The Internet is a powerful tool, and if we use it wisely, it can have a dramatic impact on helping us inspire and motivate this generation of believers to share the message of the cross with this culture. But the choice is ours. We can use it to build up, or use it to tear down.

Writer Jason Morehead put it this way:

"The same questions should be considered by us all: Are we using the powerful, disruptive technology at our own fingertips to encourage, to think critically and compassionately, to spread shalom and create a 'meaningful society'? Or are we using it to sow seeds of discord and hatred, spread vitriol and thoughtlessness, and give license to our own pride and avarice?"

That's a pretty good question as we begin our journey . . .

— 2 —

BRANDING AND POSITIONING

"As a child, I used to wonder why markets in my locality were all situated near the main roads. I grew up a little to get the answer; 'business minded people can meet there easily!' Your dream must be situated where it can meet people!"

—Israelmore Ayivor

A generation ago, all a preacher or teacher needed to be successful in ministry was a calling, a working knowledge of the Bible, and a good set of lungs. It didn't take much back then, and great ministries were sometimes built with little more than a drivable car and a passion for sharing the gospel.

Today it's different. Pastors, evangelists, and ministry leaders struggle under one of the most frustrating and competitive cultural influencers in history—the power of global media. It is obvious that the media's influence on our lives is pervasive, and education, business, religion, leisure, science, and even family life are all measured against that influence.

That's why the greatest challenge you face is how to effectively express your ministry in a media-dominated, consumer-oriented culture. How can people hear you and your message alongside the maddening swirl of media "clutter"—TV, radio, computers, mobile devices, the Internet, and other technologies competing for our attention? How do we get the message of the Church heard through the massive and growing wave of media static?

Cut through the clutter.

The truth is, the message you have to share is the greatest of all time. Advertisers clamor for attention over what they pitch as a "can't miss" product, and yours truly is. And yet to get people's attention takes an understanding of how to cut through the overwhelming media clutter, as well as connecting and then developing meaningful relationships with our congregations, supporters, or audiences. We need to move far beyond traditional communication techniques and create a powerful strategy for reaching the most distracted audience in the history of the world.

It's about getting your message heard. It's about telling your story and making that story connect with an audience. In a world where perception is just as important as reality, how can we position ourselves to make an impact?

DO YOU STAND OUT?

People look at branding in different ways. Many say it's a promise a brand makes to a customer. For instance, the National Football League's promise is "To be the premier sports and entertainment brand that brings people together, connecting them socially and emotionally like no other." Coca-Cola promises "To inspire moments of optimism and uplift." For Richard Branson's Virgin family of companies it's "To be genuine, fun, contemporary, and different in everything we do at a reasonable price." Automaker BMW promises to be "The ultimate driving machine."

I think of branding more from the perspective of "positioning." From that angle a brand is really a story that surrounds a person, organization, or product. In other words, in a world of incredible choice, what makes you or your message different? How can you stand out and be noticed? Why should someone pause and consider what you have to say?

What do people think of when they think of you, your church, or your ministry?

In my book *Unique: Telling Your Story in the Age of Brands and Social Media*, I highlight keys for successful branding and identity, and those same elements can be adapted and applied for ministering in this media-driven culture. Among them are a few things most pastors need to consider:

Visibility is just as important as ability.

As harsh as it may sound, the truth is that being seen in this cluttered culture is a big step toward being effective. Tragically, there are thousands of brilliant, gifted pastors and leaders who will never make an impact because people don't know who they are.

As a producer in Hollywood, I see this clearly illustrated when actors of little ability and skill make millions of dollars just because they were in the right place at the right time. At the same time at casting sessions, I'm amazed at the incredible level of talent among unknown actors. There are men and women with amazing gifts who will never be recognized or known.

In ministry, the people you see on national TV or listen to on the radio aren't necessarily the most gifted, anointed, or skilled ministry leaders out there. But they have influence because they have visibility. Is it fair? Absolutely not. But neither was the Roman occupation during the early Church, or many other cultural contexts church leaders have confronted throughout history.

Does ability matter? No question about it. I believe in education, skill, expertise, calling, and personal growth. When the door opens, you'd better be ready to act and have the talent and calling to back it up.

But unless that door opens, all the talent in the world will do little outside of entertaining your family. Getting your face out there isn't necessarily the act of an egotistical maniac. Certainly there are narcissists in the media and a few on religious television. But the truth is, getting on the radar of the public is the first step toward understanding the power of getting your message heard.

Perception is just as important as reality.

In a world where social media, mobile phones, and other technologies spread the word at light speed, the first impression matters. In the past, it was all about *facts*, but today it's about *perception*. For instance, it doesn't matter if you're an anointed man or woman of God if people think you're a con artist.

Someone once said that if you don't control your perception, you'll live the rest of your life at the mercy of others who will. Who will write the story of your life and ministry? Will you leave your own legacy, or will you wait for others to create it for you? Who you are is important, but you can also never underestimate the value of how you are perceived.

Being different is critical.

A quick look at Christian churches and organizations will prove that most are similar in their look, style, and presentation. But the world isn't looking for another famous pastor or ministry leader. People are looking for someone different and original. That doesn't mean that you preach or teach a different gospel, but God gave you unique DNA, so your job is to discover how your unique gifts and talents can differentiate the way you share that message from everyone else.

You have no idea the number of pastors who call our offices each week and ask us to "do the same thing for us that you did for your national ministry clients." They've got it backward. There's already one of them. A new person needs to emphasize his unique differences.

In working with many of our clients, I'm reminded of the artist Michelangelo, who was asked how he carved such brilliant statues of angels. He remarked that he didn't carve statues; he just removed the excess stone so the angel inside could come out.

That's often the case with the work our team does for numerous clients. It's not so much a matter of recreating or building a ministry; it's more about cutting away the junk so the real ministry that's inside can be released. And believe me, the junk is there. Lack of professionalism, poor media production, unqualified staff, poor taste, inept leadership, insecurity, small budgets, bad assumptions, poor decisions from the past, a confusing story, and more plague many organizations today and hamper their effectiveness.

What's your story?

Few men and women in the ministry world are truly unique and different. God is the great Creator, and yet most ministry leaders simply copy what they see on TV or hear on a podcast. Listen to the old Apple computer ads and "think different." God created you as a unique individual, so what does that mean for the type of vision you're called to accomplish and the people you're called to reach?

Whatever the size of your current crowd, these are essential insights that will help you create a compelling brand that can impact your ministry and help you make a connection that could potentially influence the world.

UNIFYING YOUR CHURCH OR MINISTRY BRAND COULD SAVE TENS OF THOUSANDS OF DOLLARS . . . AND A LOT OF CONFUSION.

Fast Company magazine recently reported that leaders from the city of Oslo, Norway, discovered they were spending $5 million a year because so many divisions and departments of city government had their own logo and brand. As *Fast Company* put it:

> When the city of Oslo audited its books recently, it found something unsettling. With 50,000 government employees working in over

200 organizations, it was paying 40 million kroner a year—or about $5 million—for agencies to spend on new logos and updated brand guidelines. That's because every organization within Oslo had its own identity, and some had a few; the official count of bespoke logos exceeded 250 in all.

Years ago I worked with a large church that literally had sixty different logos and brands throughout the organization. Everyone had a logo—the missions outreach, the youth ministry, the sports ministry, the seniors—even the parking team had their own logo. Not only was it costing a lot of money (keep in mind that each of those departments was billing the church to design and update those new logos, and some were having brand guidelines created like Oslo was doing), but even worse—it was creating enormous confusion throughout the community about the church's actual perception.

So the first thing I did as a creative consultant was to unify all those departments around a single church brand. Sure they could each have some variation, but at least they all had a unified look and style that was immediately recognizable as being part of that particular church. As a result, the recognizability of the church skyrocketed in the surrounding community.

Think about it in your own church or ministry. Do you have a unified look and style that people recognize is from your particular church or ministry? If not, then I strongly recommend you rethink your overall brand and perception.

In a cluttered world, perception matters, as the city of Oslo discovered:

Money savings was only one part of the project's appeal—and that the update was a necessary public service. The city was also aware, through polling, that citizens were confused by the multitudes of brands, unsure of where the government ended and private and nonprofit sectors began. It was very difficult to understand what the city does: "How is my tax money spent?" In other words, the rebrand doesn't just save the city of Oslo money. It proves the government's value to its citizens, too.

How can you improve your church or ministry's value by changing its perception with the public?

MARTIN LUTHER: THE BRAND

A fascinating example of the power of an effective brand is the story of reformer Martin Luther. The story is well documented in the book by Andrew Pettegree, *Brand Luther: How an Unheralded Monk Turned His Small Town into a Center of Publishing, Made Himself the Most Famous Man in Europe—and Started the Protestant Reformation*. It's a long title, but worth the time.

The year 2017 was the 500th anniversary of the Protestant Reformation, and that year I had the opportunity to film documentary footage for the *Museum of the Bible* in Wittenberg, Germany—the famous town where legend says Luther nailed his 95 Theses to the door of the local church. As we wrestle with the issues surrounding our digital age, it's fascinating to see how this relatively unknown monk used the emerging platform of publishing to his advantage. European publishing exploded largely because of the popularity of Luther's writings, but few people know just how much Luther was involved in the technology of printing.

He personally supervised his publishing, refused to deal with shoddy printers, and instinctively understood the power of high-quality design. He also experimented with different lengths of books—from very short pamphlets (since the printer's investment was small) to longer, full length books. In fact, his brilliance is evident in three key decisions:

When the vast majority of theological writing was done in Latin, Luther chose to write in German, the language of the people. That made his work available to anyone who was literate, and created a sensation. One of the big reasons he won the day against his critics was that so many of them wrote in Latin, which would reach church leaders, but not the wider public. And yet today, a significant number of Christian leaders write for academic publishers, or use jargon that regular people have difficulty understanding. Where are the masses today? On social media, watching short videos, or streaming content, and most pastors are completely ignoring those platforms.

His decision to write short. A remarkable amount of his total output was pamphlet-sized works—quick to print, cheap to buy, and easy to carry and read. An English parallel was William Tyndale's decision to print his New Testament as a small pocket-sized edition. Since it was illegal to own a Bible in English, hiding it in a pocket was a big reason for its popularity. Luther and Tyndale weren't just focused on the content, they understood that packaging was critical.

Likewise, today the most influential people in the entertainment industry are YouTube stars—men and women who produce five- to ten-minute programs in their parent's basement or a spare bedroom. They understand the power of "short" and as a result, are reaching millions of people.

His partnership with artist Lucas Cranach virtually assured that the cover designs of all his work would be noticed. At the time, few understood the importance of cover art, but Luther realized the power of perception and formed a design partnership with one of the most influential artists of his time.

Legendary designer Jonathan Ive led the design team at Apple for nearly three decades. From day one, founder Steve Jobs understood the influence of design, and many inside Apple have suggested Ive was the second most influential voice in the company, only behind Jobs himself. Few would argue that the compelling design of Apple products was one of the most important reasons for their success.

The great paradox of Luther's life is that printing was essential to the creation of Martin Luther, while at the same time, Martin Luther was a powerful force in shaping the publishing industry in Germany and beyond. It's a fascinating story of how Luther used the media to reach the greatest number of people, and in the process, changed the direction of Christianity.

Perhaps more than anything, it is a compelling challenge for us to have a similar vision and determination to reach this culture in our age of digital media.

OK, I GET IT. SO SHOULD I HIRE A BRANDING EXPERT?

When I wrote my original book on branding called *Branding Faith* in 2008, the word "branding" had hardly been uttered inside a church or other Christian organizations. In fact, the amount of criticism I endured just trying to start the conversation was enormous. People didn't want to believe the power of perception or identity and the role it played in getting people to listen to your message, buy your product, or donate to your cause. But since that time, things have changed, and not always in a good way.

Today, "branding agencies" that specialize in churches and ministries have sprung up across the country and don't seem to be slowing down. Nearly everyone I talk to these days is either a "branding expert" or a "social media expert." (And I say that with only a tiny smirk.)

The bottom line is that for a few, to justify high fees and make themselves look serious, many have jumped through amazing hoops and created a lengthy process to "discover" your brand. As a result, many church leaders end up with a huge bill and massive reports they don't even understand. One major national ministry called me recently to tell me they spent $250,000 on a branding study, which resulted in a 1,200 page document, and they had absolutely no clue what to do with it.

It's tragic actually (this is donor money), and sometimes it seems like a few are turning the concept of branding into a religion itself. But the truth is, the key to an effective brand is to define the perception you have in the marketplace and work from there. It's understanding the promise you're making to your community, your customers, or your donors. It's trying to positively influence the story that surrounds you, your organization, or product.

Branding should be a tool that helps you share your story more effectively. It influences your perception and helps cut through the clutter of multiple messages to tell that story. What it shouldn't become is a one size fits all solution. Plus, no branding study, brand statement, or logo design will overcome bad preaching at a church, or poor performance at a nonprofit.

Your story is bound up in the unique quality of
your content, your DNA, and the confidence
that comes from acting in your strengths.

A great branding study will help you discover your strengths, your unique story, and help you express it well. But if your organization is dysfunctional or if the leadership is failing, spending money to enhance your brand is only putting a new coat of paint on a car with no engine.

I still believe in the power of branding.

Is there a process? Yes.

Is there an investment? Yes.

Does it matter? Yes.

In fact, in 2012 I updated and rewrote *Branding Faith* into *Unique: Telling Your Story in the Age of Brands and Social Media*. I needed to include social media, which hadn't been invented when I wrote the original, as well as update the book with changes happening in the media and culture.

Branding is the key to break through
the media clutter, and allows you to connect
with your audience and supporters.

The point? Learn to tell your story more effectively. It's the key to breaking through the media clutter that surrounds us, and allows you to connect with your audience and your supporters.

While there are plenty of reputable branding agencies out there, there's plenty of others who have a lot of show, but no go. Get recommendations from other churches and ministries. Do your homework. Make sure whoever you pick is a right fit for your team and your vision.

Because the only thing worse than not telling your story at all is telling it poorly.

KEY PRINCIPLES TO CONSIDER ABOUT BRANDING AND POSITIONING:

1. **Terms like "marketing," "branding," or "positioning" are not bad words.** It's simply the act of making your product or message available to the largest possible audience. In that context, strategies like this should become a priority for all Christian leaders.

2. **When it comes to communication, clutter is real.** For your message to stand out, you need to rise above the noise, and the best way to accomplish that is to be unique.

3. **You were put on the earth for a reason, so start with your own gifts and talents.** What about your calling, skills, or gifts make you unique? Is it your style of communication and delivery? Is it your creativity? Is it your leadership? Is it your unique perspective on teaching or preaching? Is it your expertise? Whatever it is, use that to rise above the noise and get your message noticed.

4. **A logo is not a brand.** A logo is the physical expression of your brand story. So start with how you believe your church, your ministry, and you are perceived in the minds of the public. What is the story that surrounds you and your ministry? What do people think of when they think of you? In many ways it's a promise that you're making to your congregation, your audience, or your community.

5. **It's not "either/or."** We have to deliver on our promises, so make sure you have expertise in scripture, and your walk with God is solid. But at the same time, spend more and more effort on how to get your message heard by more people. It's really the Great Commission, and while in today's cluttered and noisy world it's more difficult than ever, it can also be much more effective than ever.

— 3 —

SPEAKING TO A DIGITAL GENERATION

"I grew up in a physical world, and I speak
English. The next generation is growing up in a
digital world, and they speak social."

—Angela Ahrendts

Your voice is your most important tool, but the digital revolution is changing our language. Some might say that having a section on public speaking in a book for pastors and ministry leaders is a waste of space. After all, you speak for a living and probably don't need many tips in that area. However, it's important to realize one important thing:

Public speaking has changed in a digital world.

In this section I'll cover some technological issues like using an iPad or other mobile device for your notes, how to master presentation software like PowerPoint or Keynote, and what you should know if you want to expand your career by speaking at conferences or other events outside your church or ministry.

However, just as crucial to understanding these topics is the realization that the audience has changed as well. In a world of shortened attention spans, how can we still capture people's attention? When an audience is obsessed by mobile devices, is it possible to still break through?

TEN SECRETS TO IMPROVE YOUR PUBLIC SPEAKING IN A DIGITAL AGE

Even if you're not a preacher, if you're going to go very far as a leader or creative professional, sooner or later you'll need to speak to audiences. Whether it's a conference keynote, workshop, or you just need to inspire your team at the office, I believe every leader should be comfortable speaking in front of a group. However, there are plenty of speakers, preachers, and teachers who simply aren't capable of captivating an audience. That's why I created these top ten secrets that will take your public speaking to a new level. Conquer this list and you're on your way:

1. **Stop using "fill in" words like "um," "like," or "aaah."** Seriously. Stop it. In today's noisy and cluttered world, speakers feel like they need to fill the empty spaces in their talk. But in that deafening world, we actually value silence. So don't be afraid to pause. When you don't know what to say, don't insert nonsensical "filler" words—simply pause and think. Better yet, know your talk so well that you won't stumble.

Listen to yourself speaking and you'll discover all kinds of filler words. I say the word "incredible" way too much. Others say "again" over and over. Eliminate any words you use repetitiously or those that have no real meaning in your sentence. In my opinion, few things make a speaker look more amateur than using filler words, so cut it out if you're serious about speaking.

2. **Don't get obsessed with your notes.** Occasionally checking your notes is fine, but referring to your notes too often is the best way to tell your audience you're not prepared. If you need to read your talk, then print it out and pass it around because I'd rather read a message myself then have a speaker do it. Practice, learn your talk, get comfortable with it, and stop constantly looking down and checking your notes.

3. Don't let unexpected things throw you off balance. I've spoken to live audiences hundreds of times, and problems happen more often than you think. The sound goes out, lighting glitches happen, microphones cut out, there's a crazy person in the audience, or more often there's a technical problem using PowerPoint or Keynote. At one event a set piece fell over on the stage during my talk. Always expect the unexpected and don't let it ruffle you or throw you off. Make a joke about it and move on.

4. Be very careful about using PowerPoint. See my tips later in this chapter or read the book by Nick Morgan, *Give Your Speech, Change the World: How to Move Your Audience to Action.* That book begins with a simple premise: become a good speaker first, and then add PowerPoint if necessary. Too many inexperienced speakers go straight to using presentation software, and it hurts the presentation. They end up spending all their preparation time looking for slides, writing the text, and getting the order right—when they should be using that time practicing their speech. Hold off on using presentation software and focus your time on becoming a great speaker first.

5. Make eye contact with the audience. I attended a church recently where the pastor never looked at the audience. It was very curious, but more speakers than you think avoid eye contact with the people in the seats. They look at their notes, stare at the floor, or lock in on the wall behind the audience. I understand it because it took me a while to overcome being distracted by the facial expressions of audience members. But if you're going to connect with the message, you need to connect with your eyes. Look at the audience just as if you were talking to a friend. Without that relationship, you won't make an impact.

6. Make sure your "speaking voice" is the same as your normal talking voice. I have a friend who has a very nice voice, but the minute he begins speaking to an audience, he switches to the deep promotional sound of the classic "radio voice." Other people speak with a monotone and exhibit very little emotion. A good speaking voice comes with practice, and sometimes you do have to project your voice, but as much as possible, make sure it's YOUR voice, not some made up voice that you think sounds dramatic or important.

7. Don't get stuck behind the pulpit or podium. Too many speakers look like they're bolted to the floor. Great speakers move, use expressions, and speak "physically" as well as vocally.

8. Make sure you connect with the audience. This generation is about "connecting," so although there will always be audience members who fall asleep, look disinterested or bored, be on the lookout for large numbers mentally checking out. This is really about knowing your audience and understanding their expectations. I always do my best to find out ahead of the event who's in the audience, what their interests are, and why they came. Certainly you want to give them more than they expect, but start with meeting their expectations.

9. Don't lose your place in your presentation or in your notes. There are numerous ways to avoid this, and the best is simply to know your presentation. But if you're developing something new and need your notes, think about printing them in a large font that's easy to read. You should also abbreviate or outline so you're not wrestling with many pages—in fact, some speakers experiment with colorful circles, arrows, and other indicators. As you practice, look away from time to time and then back to see if you can easily find your place again in your notes. Getting lost is a strong signal that you're not prepared, and you'll quickly lose credibility.

10. If the audience looks bored or people start leaving early, you're in trouble. Of course, this is your worst nightmare, and if it happens in big numbers there's no real fix because it's simply too late. Either you've missed their expectations or not been interesting or professional enough for them to stick with you to the end. My advice is more practice. Go back to the beginning of this list and start over before your next talk.

Bonus: I have to admit that even after speaking at hundreds of keynotes, workshops, and other sessions, I still don't fully understand audiences. Sometimes I'll see people who look absolutely bored (even angry), but after the talk they'll come up in tears telling me how my message changed their life. Others who are on the edge of their seat during my talk, quickly walk out the door as soon as it's over. Understand there will always be outliers that you won't figure out. However, it's the larger group that should be your focus. Do your jokes get a laugh? Is the audience attentive during your serious moments? Are they taking notes? If you can win the greater group, and do it with consistency, then you know you're on the right track.

EVERY PASTOR COULD BE A BETTER PREACHER OR SPEAKER

Deep down, every preacher knows that it's the power of the Holy Spirit that convicts—not the eloquence of the preaching. However, that scriptural truth doesn't give us an excuse to preach without skill, passion, and conviction. Whether you're like William Booth, founder of the Salvation Army preaching on a street corner, or you wear a fine robe in a magnificent sanctuary, or you're somewhere in between, it's your task and great calling to preach the gospel to the absolute best of your ability. John Wesley said, "Give me one hundred preachers who fear nothing but sin and desire nothing but God; such alone will shake the gates of hell."

And yet I travel to church after church watching pastors preach with shockingly little skill and even less passion. The sad truth is that there are too many pulpits across this country filled with preachers and teachers who simply aren't capable of captivating an audience.

Beyond the starting point of a preacher's calling and personal commitment to Christ, there are also practical skills that can make a dramatic difference in communicating your message. In today's digital age, there are three particular areas I believe would literally transform your impact in the pulpit and elsewhere:

Use your creative team. If you pastor a large enough church to have a creative team (or at the least a single creative designer or communication person), then use them. Pastors tend to shoulder the burden of too many things beyond writing the sermon and leading the church—such as thinking of compelling sermon titles, promoting a series, writing up something for the bulletin, getting the message out on social media, etc. Bring your creative person or team into the conversation early and let them help. Research indicates the average adult makes about thirty-five thousand decisions a day, and there's even a clinical term called "Decision Fatigue." Stop being a lone wolf and get some creative help.

Be more confident physically. This year I saw too many pastors who looked like they were embarrassed to be in the pulpit. They didn't stand up straight, look poised, or even give the impression they knew what they were talking about. It's not about faking it; it's about building up the congregation's confidence in the message you're sharing. Think of how often people responded to the teachings of Jesus as *someone who had authority*. They won't respond if they don't believe what you're saying.

Lastly, understand that your message is the "point of the spear." In other words, the message of every communication platform from the church should trickle down from the Sunday sermon. I see far too many churches where the pastor preaches one message, but the website, the social media, and other communication platforms all say something different. Marketing guru Seth Godin says, "We remember the things we see again and again." That means the familiar is remembered and trusted. So make sure that the week following your message, that message is reflected over and over in all the communication that flows out from the church.

As a preacher of the gospel in today's culture we often have it backwards. Philosopher and theologian Soren Kierkegaard got it right when he said, "People have an idea that the preacher is an actor on a stage and they are the critics, blaming or praising him. What they don't know is that they are the actors on the stage; he (the preacher) is merely the prompter standing in the wings, reminding them of their lost lines."

Your job "reminding them of their lost lines" could not be more important, so do everything in your power to set the stage where your congregation is ready to be convicted and transformed by the power of the gospel.

THE SECRETS OF MAKING GREAT PRESENTATIONS

Every day, someone in America is damaging their career, and it happens behind a pulpit or podium. Respected men and women—often excellent leaders—end up dying a horrible death in front of an audience, usually at a ministry conference, corporate meeting, or workshop. It doesn't take a CSI officer from the crime lab to analyze the evidence from the scene. It can easily be found in an audience filled with people nodding off to sleep, checking their e-mail, mumbling to themselves, or finding excuses to leave early.

The truth is, most speaker mistakes could easily be solved with a few easy steps—keys that only take a short time to learn, but could literally catapult your speaking career to an entirely new level. And since so many pastors ask me about how to expand their speaking to major conferences, here's a list to consider carefully. It might save you from the dreaded "ECH" (Early Career Humiliation).

Workshop, Conference, or Sermon Titles:

1. Titles are critically important for their advertising and promotional value, so I suggest you make it "provocative" but not "cute." "Provocative" simply means *compelling*. Intrigue the audience and pique their interest. Create a desire for the subject. The workshop name should create a "buzz" and get people talking about it long before they even arrive. But don't get cute or try too hard, or you'll end up embarrassing yourself. I especially encourage people to be cautious using "parodies" (trying to co-op the name of a popular song, TV show, or movie).

2. Keep it short. A title like: "My life as a missionary with a limited financial budget and wacky family in the remote jungle of Uganda" doesn't really have an impact. Keep the main title short and sweet, and use a sub-title if necessary to convey more information about the workshop.

3. When it comes to titles, be careful with humor; it can easily backfire. (Enough said.)

Workshop Content:

1. Avoid information overload. A great presentation is 70 percent INSPI-RATION, and 30 percent INFORMATION. Nothing is more boring than information overload. I once had a college professor who walked into class, opened a notebook, and simply read word for word for the entire hour. He never looked up, not even once. Then the bell would ring, and he'd close the notebook and walk out the door. No questions, no conversation, no relationship. Worst professor I ever had.

2. Don't duplicate the written word. At my media workshops, I will often provide a handout with detailed information, reading lists, or research references. That allows me to use the time in front of the crowd to inspire them, motivate them, and help them enjoy the experience. I want to create a passion in the participants for the subject. So limit the amount of heavy information. That's not to say you can't give out important facts at a confer-ence—just keep it in balance. People would rather read it later than listen to you read it for them.

3. Avoid the slide crutch. I'm very careful about using slide presenta-tions—probably because I've seen them used so badly. Too many speakers today rely on programs like PowerPoint and Keynote to cover their poor speaking skills, and believe me, the audience notices. As I said earlier, learn first to be an engaging speaker, and only use "devices" as a supplement to an already fascinating presentation.

But if you do make the decision to use programs like PowerPoint or Keynote, here are a few tips:

Keep it visual. Once again, use a preprinted handout if you're giving out too much written information. Slide content should be simple and easy to understand.

Don't forget white space. Too much text crammed into a slide is difficult to read. Keep the slides simple and easy to follow.

Take the time to find interesting pictures and illustrations. Don't rely on the stick figures or simple illustrations that came with the program. We've seen them a hundred times already. Be original, be creative, be different. And please avoid cheesy stock footage!

Don't create a slide unless it's absolutely crucial to understanding the point. Otherwise, it just creates clutter and distracts from your message.

Make sure the slides have visual continuity. Use the same or similar backgrounds, font styles, and overall graphic design throughout the presentation. Otherwise, each slide will look like it came from a different presentation. Give your talk a finished, professional look, and if possible, have custom backgrounds created that reflect your subject, your brand, or your organization.

Be ready for technical malfunctions. First, triple check before the event to make sure what you need to present will be provided. Next, have a backup copy of the presentation on a thumb drive or website so you can use another computer if yours crashes. Finally, show up at the room early to work out any plug, adapter, or equipment issues.

Be careful giving out copies of the presentation to the audience. If you're building a personal brand or career as an expert on the subject, I would give out a handout rather than a copy of the actual presentation. Especially if this is how you make a living, you may not want people stealing your thunder by using the presentation you worked so hard to develop, so be careful about giving it to others.

For Speaking at Conference Sessions or Workshops:

Find out who's in the audience. I always ask the organizers long before the event who's registering, and at the event I often ask it again to the audience themselves. During my media workshops, I need to know if I'm speaking to producers, directors, video editors, actors, pastors, ministry leaders, or civilians. I want to know if they're professionals or students, experienced or novice. Don't shoot in the dark. Know your audience and focus your message to that specific target.

The "panel paradox." Most conferences love panels, because it allows more speakers to participate. Theoretically, it provides more perspectives and expertise, and allows the conference to keep feelings from being hurt by giving more people speaking opportunities. If you're the host, it also allows you to give out "favors" to friends, clients, and associates by bringing them to the table. However, in a typical hour workshop, with four to five panelists, after a few minutes of welcome and some Q&A at the end, each panelist is left with only five to ten minutes to actually share. That's why panels *seem* effective, but rarely are. They don't allow any one speaker to actually go deeply into a subject, and as a result, most panel presentations or discussions are pretty shallow. Sure it might help you score a few points by adding more speakers, but in my experience, most panels leave the audience frustrated and feeling shortchanged.

The interview format. There are various reasons to invite a speaker—sometimes it's for his or her expertise or experience, and other times it's because of their new book, movie, or other accomplishment. However, none of those reasons make them a good speaker. If you're afraid your guest might be boring or uncomfortable in front of an audience, consider turning it into an interview rather than a formal speech. In other words, set up two stools or tall director's chairs, and you take the lead by interviewing them in front of the audience. First, it puts them at ease, and second, it allows you to control the presentation. I've discovered that interviews often allow us a more intimate look at the expert, because he or she feels more relaxed and comfortable, not having to be in the lead. It also increases your chances of engaging a higher level leader at your event because they won't have to prepare for a formal talk.

Don't forget the Q&A. The best way to help your audience is often to allow them time for questions. No matter how great your presentation, you can't possibly address all the particular challenges the audience members are facing, so I always enjoy hearing from the crowd. I've discovered that if you handle it right, the question and answer time can be far more informative than the actual presentation. Think of it this way—the presentation builds the foundation, and the Q&A customizes the home.

Don't be commercial. There are a few things worse than a workshop speaker who spends his or her time promoting a product or discussing themselves. Certainly we want to hear about your experience as it relates to the subject, but we didn't pay all this money to hear you toot your own horn. Be respectful of the audience and focus on helping *them*. Plant that seed into their lives, and it will come back to you many times over. One self-promotion technique that works well is the handout. Don't be afraid to put your contact information on the handout—especially if you'd like people to reach out to you for more information after the event.

Finally—keep it moving! We live in a sound-bite, digital, ADHD world, so don't lose your audience with a boring presentation. Keep it lively with emotion and excitement. Without going overboard, move around the stage, be dramatic with your voice, and be fun and compelling. Object lessons can help, so think about items that would help visually explain your points.

Workshops and conferences can be an incredibly important time to develop your personal brand, or promote your ideas about particular issues. Don't waste the opportunity. Practice in front of a mirror, bring a friend to help with technical issues, and more than anything, come prepared. A great presentation can dramatically change your perception, and reposition you to a far greater audience.

SHOULD YOU USE A TABLET OR OTHER MOBILE DEVICE FOR SPEAKING NOTES?

I love technology and I applaud speakers, preachers, teachers, and others who use a mobile device for speaking notes. But as much I want people to know we're savvy with technology, here are a few cautions I'm seeing a lot out there on podiums, pulpits, and classrooms:

1. Speakers tend to hunch over when using a tablet. I watched a teacher recently spend his entire talk hunched over the podium looking at his tablet like the hunchback of Notre Dame. You can see paper notes from every angle and direction, but it's not so easy with a tablet. Hunched over, you look like you're in your own little world and not interested in the audience.

2. **Speakers tend to lose eye contact with the audience when using a tablet.** It's a smaller space than a piece of paper so you tend to turn pages more often and struggle to keep track of where you are on the screen. As a result, you lose eye contact with the audience, and when you do that, you lose them.

3. **Speakers can look inept with the technology.** In your effort to look tech savvy, it often backfires. Let's face it—a tablet can be tricky in front of an audience. Text moves, pages turn, documents close, notes disappear. I can't tell you how many times I've suffered through a speaker saying, "Hang on, I've lost my place," or "Where did it go? I had it right here," or "Whoops, I think I've lost my talk," or "Hey (insert assistant's name here), can you come up and help me find my notes?"

Here are some solutions to help you feel more confident and comfortable with notes on mobile devices:

1. **Practice, practice, practice.** Get as comfortable with a tablet or phone as you are with note cards or paper.

2. **Take the time to learn how to stop the rotation, hold the page, increase or decrease the font size, set the screen saver, and much more.** Also, find a .pdf reader or other notes app that you're comfortable using. Make sure the settings won't betray you in front of a crowd.

3. **Learn to hold it well.** Get a partial cover with a gripping back so it stays in your hand. Learn where the buttons and the on-screen navigation tools are so you don't hit them by mistake.

4. **Learn to keep eye contact with the audience.** Don't let a tablet pin you to the lectern or keep your eyes away from the audience. Your goal should be to make the tablet invisible. If the audience becomes fixated on your poor handling of the device, that means they're not paying attention to you or your message.

A tablet can be a powerful tool for speakers, so learn to use it well.

HOW TO LAUNCH YOUR CAREER AS A SPEAKER BEYOND YOUR CHURCH

You may already be preaching and teaching to a local church, but perhaps you have a desire to expand your speaking opportunities. As you grow to larger and larger venues, bigger audiences can be terrifying or exhilarating, depending on the event, your preparation, and your skill as a speaker. Because you're speaking to a group, it's a fantastic opportunity to cast a vision, enhance your reputation, and make an impact with your message, so doing it well is vital.

But if you're a pastor, then keep in mind that this isn't your congregation. They may not know you and won't be as forgiving as your home church—especially if it's a younger audience. That's why of all the issues we've discussed, these are five key principles worth remembering:

1. Respect the audience. Perhaps you're speaking because of a new book you've written, project you've accomplished, area of expertise, or something else you're passionate about. Whatever the reason, make sure that topic is the subject they've come to hear. Too often less experienced conference speakers and preachers try to shoehorn their topic to fit any audience and it simply doesn't work.

Become almost obsessed with finding out who your audience is ahead of time and focus your topic on that particular group and their expectations. And while you're at it, be as specific as possible:

-> *Is the audience made up of students? What age? What interests? Why did they come?*

-> *Is the audience made up of leaders? What kind? What level? What business or nonprofit area?*

-> *Are they professionals? What level? What challenges are they facing?*

-> *Is this a secular or faith-based event?*

-> *Is the audience made up of a mix of attendees? If so, discover as much as you can about the mix.*

–> *And don't forget the theme of the conference. In most cases, your topic should be in line with the event's overall theme.*

This information will allow you to tailor your content to exactly that audience and when it happens, your chances of being remembered will skyrocket.

2. Be interesting to watch. No matter how great your content, if you spend the time hugging the podium while staring at your notes, you won't be a compelling speaker. Be physically interesting. Move. Be expressive. Look the audience in the eye. Don't force it, but be natural like you'd talk to a friend. You wouldn't sit frozen staring at your coffee cup at Starbucks with a buddy, so don't do it to an audience.

3. Be careful with jokes. There are great speakers out there who are funny, and there are just as many great speakers who aren't. If comedy comes naturally to you, great, but if it doesn't, don't try to force it. There's nothing worse than watching someone who isn't funny try to make a lame joke. There's no shame in not being a comedian, so don't feel guilty about it. Just stay in your lane and express the personality God gave you.

4. Never go beyond your time limit. I generally finish a talk a few minutes early, because I'd rather people want more than be upset because I went too long. At most conferences and events, the clock matters, because the daily schedule features other events after yours. So no matter how important you feel your message is, once you go over your allotted time, it can create all kinds of problems behind the scenes. I know good speakers who rarely get invited anymore because they've abused the clock so often in the past.

5. Learn to deal with not being invited to some events. You're excited. You're called to a purpose. You enjoy speaking. You have something to say that people need to hear. I get it, but it may take time to be invited to major conferences and events. I've been doing this for decades and there are still plenty of events where I haven't yet been invited to speak. I don't worry about it—I just focus on the places and events that are interested in me right now.

Not being invited isn't a personal thing or a slight against you—there are many reasons why you may not be right for a particular event—your area of expertise, fitting in with the other speaker's subjects, the conference theme, timing—and the fact that they simply may not know you, or your subject area.

The best way to get on the radar is to reconsider how you position yourself. Perhaps you weren't invited because they're confused about your area of expertise, so clearly defining your perception and positioning should be a major priority for you. You'll become a better speaker when you stop being upset at not being invited to some events, and spend that time working hard to become amazing at the places that invite you.

THE LONGER THE SPEAKER BIO THE LESS EXPERIENCED THE SPEAKER

Let me know if you've seen this rule in action: *Novice or less experienced conference speakers have the longest biography in the conference program.* I was guilty of this for years because I was desperate to make people think I was worthy of speaking at the event. I wanted to impress people. (I admit it.) But I started noticing major speakers have the shortest biography in the program. Why?

They don't need to impress anyone. If they've written books or been in ministry for years, or have a track record, they don't need to show off in their speaker bio. And while you're at it, have a little fun with it. Here's the bio for my friend Jonathan Bock, founder and CEO of motion picture marketing and public relations firm Grace Hill Media:

Jonathan Bock is the founder and president of Grace Hill Media. Mr. Bock began his career in publicity at Warner Bros. Prior to that, he was a sitcom writer, widely regarded throughout the industry as "not very good." Mr. Bock serves on the board of Reel Spirituality at Fuller Theological Seminary and is a deacon at Bel Air Presbyterian Church. Father of two beautiful daughters, he's married to his first wife, Kelly. He also, with a few warm-up frames, can consistently bowl in the low nineties.

It tells you who he is, what he does, and that he doesn't take himself too seriously. You can have a longer bio on your website or resume, but when it comes to speaking events, conferences, or seminars, don't bore the audience with the details, or give them your life story.

A great speaker biography is a teaser. It's not meant to impress the audience; it's meant to make them want to hear more.

WHY THE SOUND ENGINEER IS SO IMPORTANT TO A SPEAKER

I almost didn't include this, but I think it's a very important observation. Everyone knows a good audio engineer is important to a speaker because great sound is vital to the success of a presentation. That's why professional speakers, teachers, or pastors invest in a professional sound crew whenever possible. But there's another—perhaps even more important—reason that a good sound person is indispensable:

He or she is often the last person a speaker talks to before taking the stage.

I speak at conferences and events around the world, so I get a pretty good idea of what matters to speakers—particularly in unusual or new situations—and here's what I've found: Sound professionals are critically important to the emotional well-being of a speaker. In some situations, he or she comes up to me before speaking, and just hands me a microphone. No comment, no assistance, and no advice. So especially with a headset microphone, I struggle to get it on, and then worry about whether the microphone is in the right place or not, and then wonder if it will slide around.

Not a terribly confident place to be before I walk onto the stage.

But in the best situations, a good sound professional helps me with the microphone, stays to make sure it's fitted properly (especially with a headset mic), has some tape if necessary, and answers my questions about how it works. Then he or she will often say something like, "We're very excited to hear your presentation," or "We've been waiting a long time for this event."

Motivating? You bet. Confidence building? Heck yeah.

Sound engineers? Your role is far more important than audio levels, EQ, and running a sound board.

Conference directors, pastors, and leaders? Make sure you share this with your sound team. Encourage them. Let them know what they do is important—perhaps the most vital thing that will happen before a guest preacher or speaker takes the stage.

KEY PRINCIPLES TO CONSIDER ABOUT PUBLIC SPEAKING IN A DIGITAL AGE:

1. **Every leader (including pastors and ministry leaders) could become a better speaker.** For many leaders, your ability to speak in front of an audience is your most important tool. So develop it, and be the best you could possibly be.

2. **Be very careful about using presentation software.** Too many inexperienced speakers go straight to using presentation software, and it hurts the presentation. They end up spending all their preparation time looking for slides, writing the text, and getting the order right—when they should be using that time practicing their speech. Hold off on using PowerPoint or Keynote, and focus your time on becoming a great speaker first.

3. **Pastors, never forget that your message is the "point of the spear."** The message of every communication platform from the church should trickle down from the Sunday sermon. Make sure that the week following your message, that message is reinforced again and again in all the communication that flows out from the church.

4. **Don't carry the creative burden by yourself.** Use a creative associate or your team to help you find illustrations, stories, and do other background research. Bring your creative person or team into the conversation early so you can stop being a lone wolf and get some creative help.

5. **If you decide to use a tablet or mobile device for your sermon notes, then take the time to practice and get comfortable with the tool.** Your goal should be to make the tablet invisible. A tablet can be a powerful tool for speakers, so learn to use it well.

— 4 —

LEADING CREATIVE PEOPLE

"Leadership is the art of giving people a platform for spreading ideas that work."
—Seth Godin

In many ways, the future of media in today's digital age is the future of leading creative people. One thing about media is that it's difficult to create a social media campaign, record a podcast, produce video, live stream, create television programs, or publish books by yourself. Eventually you'll need to surround yourself with a team of creative people.

Does that mean you have to be amazingly creative yourself? Not really, but you do need to understand the principles of leading creative people, and in the process, it doesn't hurt to sharpen your own creativity as well.

Some time ago, *Bloomberg Businessweek* reported: "According to a new survey of 1,500 chief executives conducted by IBM's Institute for Business Value, CEOs identify 'creativity' as the most important leadership competency for the successful enterprise of the future." Talk to many leaders about the most important leadership competency, and you'll usually hear about financial expertise, organizational skill, or motivational ability. But the truth is—especially during this disruptive digital economy today—creativity is more and more in demand.

Now don't try and tell me that you're not creative. The truth is, we're all born creative. Just check out the toddler's class at your church next Sunday and show me a little kid who isn't wildly creative. But for whatever reason, somewhere around school age, most people's creative instincts start to recede.

If you're a leader, start tapping into your creative side once again. Management expertise, financial acumen, vision—all those things are important, but to answer the challenges we face today, creativity is becoming more and more valuable (read: critical).

We live in a design driven culture where technology is shifting the traditional rules of doing business. New times demand new approaches, and the creative leader will be the one who refuses to get stuck in old thinking, will challenge the status quo, and never defend bad ideas with lines like, "Well, that's the way we've always done it."

LEADERS: WHAT YOU SHOULD KNOW ABOUT YOUR TEAM

Whenever I consult with a church, ministry, or nonprofit, I always begin by looking closely at the team. Your employees are the ones who make an organization work, so learning as much as you can about them matters—and I'm often surprised at how little pastors and other leaders actually know about the personal side of their team. If you're not taking the time to know your people well, you're shortchanging your vision. Having studied teams over the years, here's a starting list of issues leaders need to know about their teams

Purpose is just as important as talent. Talent is important and I always recommend hiring the most talented people possible, but start with knowing why your people are there in the first place. Find out who's there just for a paycheck, and who's there to change the world. Knowing motivations is crucial for team chemistry and expectations.

Make sure they're in the right seats on the bus. You know the Jim Collins concept—get the right employees on the bus, make sure they're in the right seats, and then get the wrong ones off the bus. Brilliantly simple, and yet you'd be amazed at the number of organizations that make serious mistakes in all three areas. The church and ministry world abounds with employees in positions that conflict with their talent and gifts. That disconnect damages morale, because everyone else knows the employee is failing and everyone else becomes more frustrated by the day.

Know which ones are locked into the rules and which are more flexible. I've worked at organizations who are crippled because employees are so bound by the rules that they can't think outside the box. Rules and policies are important, but you also need a team that knows when to step outside the rules for a bigger purpose. You may remember United Airlines tossing a doctor off the plane in 2017—and the massive public relations disaster that followed—as a sad example of employees who never stopped to think outside the policy.

Be careful of employees who are building their own empire inside your organization. These are team members who will do anything to protect their turf. You want a team that is generous with their ideas, time, and talent, and knows how to work with others in the organization. You don't change the world by fighting for your turf.

Finally, of all your tasks as a leader, developing your team is one of the most important. You can't do everything yourself, but when you hand off responsibilities, you need to make sure it's handed to a capable, talented, and motivated employee. Taking the time every day to teach, encourage, and inspire your team will reap more benefits than you can possibly imagine.

And the opposite? If you've been in the ministry long, then you probably know at least one organization that crashed because of a renegade, bitter, angry team and the leaders who let it happen.

TEN REASONS YOU'RE NOT READY TO LEAD A CREATIVE TEAM

Too many churches, nonprofits, and ministries are filled with leaders who are terrible at leading creative people. In some cases, they were promoted to the position and understand they are out of their depth. But in most cases (in my experience) they actually believe they're good at leading creative people, when in truth, they are completely out of place. Based on working with more than a few inept creative leaders over the last few decades, here's my checklist of "Ten Reasons You're Not Ready to Lead a Creative Team":

1. **You simply don't like creative types.** You think they're not serious, undisciplined, and just weird.

2. **You don't understand why they prefer to work late at night or early in the morning.** You think they should just show up like everybody else and be done with it.

3. **You're not willing to defend their work to the people you report to.**

4. **You think creative people don't have a mind for business, so they won't understand the bigger picture or strategy.**

5. **Controlling the creative team is very important to you.**

6. **You like to micromanage their work.**

7. **You think creative people are flakey and undependable.**

8. **You think creative people have gigantic egos.**

9. **You think creative people only care about how "cool" an idea or project happens to be.**

10. **You like to take credit for their work.**

If you suffer from any of these tendencies, then it may be time to rethink your position. Because if you don't understand how creative people think, what they value, and why you need to defend their work, then you're really not ready to lead creative teams.

WHAT LEADERS GET WRONG WHEN IT COMES TO BUILDING GREAT TEAMS

Building great, creative teams is an art. Like an athletic coach, the key isn't just maximizing the talent of each member, it's also about combining that collective talent to do amazing things. Plenty of sports teams with all-star players lose to less talented teams who know how to work together. But there are five key mistakes I see leaders make over and over that keep them from building a legendary team.

We don't understand what teams are for. Leaders make decisions, and teams execute decisions. Don't get that confused. I consulted with a large nonprofit once with a leader who was uncomfortable making decisions, so he embraced what he called "team leadership." That meant he had a team of fourteen people who would literally have eight-hour meetings two to three times a week to make the smallest, most insignificant decisions. The organization was in chaos, all because the leader was afraid to make decisions himself. I love working with teams, but their greatest strength isn't *making* decisions, it's *executing* those decisions. Leaders—don't delegate your authority. Make sure you're using your team for the right thing.

We don't fire enough people. I love the quote from CEO Jack Welch— "When you don't fire underperforming members of your team, you're not only hurting the organization, you're hurting them—because you're giving them a false sense of what success is." It's not about kicking people to the curb, it's about helping them find the place where they can contribute and grow. Ultimately you have to get them out of the job they're failing at right now. And while you're at it—don't confuse "loyalty" and "competence." I love loyalty, but just because an employee is loyal doesn't mean they're actually good at their job.

We think an "open door policy" is a good thing. Actually, I imagine whoever invented the idea meant well. But the truth is, even with great teams, there comes a time when you should shut the door and get to work. We're finding that the trendy "open spaces" office concept simply isn't working. It's too loud, people don't have privacy, and it's incredibly distracting. Plus, some research indicates that when someone walks into your office and interrupts you, once they leave, it takes up to forty minutes to get back to that same level of focus you had before you were interrupted. How many interruptions like that will wreck your entire day?

Our teams are too big. Numbers can be relative, but once a creative team gets past eight or so people, it doesn't accomplish much because there are just too many opinions. Plus, in a large group it's too easy for distractions to happen as people start checking e-mails and start side conversations. I've always liked the advice from Amazon founder Jeff Bezos about the size of effective teams: "If you can't feed your team with two large pizzas in a meeting, you're in trouble."

Finally, team meetings are too long. I'll talk about this at greater length later, but for now, I've been in all-day marketing meetings and brainstorming sessions, and after a couple of hours, wanted to pull my hair out. Never forget that people are really good for about forty minutes or so and then need a break. So when it comes to meetings, get creative. Find an interesting location, lower the distraction level, help them focus, create an agenda, and perhaps most important—end on time. When it comes to long meetings I'll defer to Thomas Sowell who said: "People who enjoy meetings should not be in charge of anything."

ED CATMULL ON LEADING CREATIVE PEOPLE

Ed Catmull, former President of Pixar Animation Studios and Walt Disney Animation, and author of the book *Creativity, Inc.* (which I highly recommend), has an insightful perspective on leading creative teams—especially when it comes to micromanaging:

> It is easy to be critical of the micromanaging many managers resort to, yet we must acknowledge the rock and the hard place we often place them between. If they have to choose between meeting a deadline and some less well-defined mandate to "nurture" their people, they will pick the deadline every time. We tell ourselves that we will devote more time to our people if we, in turn, are given more slack in the schedule or budget, but somehow the requirements of the job always eat up the slack, resulting in increased pressure with even less room for error.

Given these realities, managers typically want two things: (1) for everything to be tightly controlled, and (2) to appear to be in control. But when control is the goal, it can negatively affect other parts of your culture. I've known many managers who hate to be surprised in meetings, for example, by which I mean they make it clear that they want to be briefed about any unexpected news in advance and in private. In many workplaces, it is a sign of disrespect if someone surprises a manager with new information in front of other people.

But what does this mean in practice? It means that there are pre-meetings before meetings, and the meetings begin to take on a pro forma tone. It means wasted time. It means that the employees who work with these people walk on eggshells. It means that fear runs rampant.

SECRETS TO LEADING HIGH ACHIEVERS

Ed Catmull led one of the most creative and high-achieving teams in the world, and as a leader, at some point in your career you'll have the influence, budget, and resources to build a team of creative high achievers. High achievers come in all packages and personality types, and can revolutionize organizations. However, what I find more often is that bosses discover pretty quickly they are way out of their depth when it comes to managing that kind of brilliant, high-energy team—or worse—they become intimidated by their talent. Either way, it's a crisis waiting to happen.

When you get to that point in your career—or if you're already there—here's a handful of good tips for maximizing your leadership ability with high achieving teams.

Start with yourself. High achievers respect leaders who have high standards, perform well under pressure, and can inspire teams even in the most difficult circumstances. You'll never lead high achievers well if you can't lead yourself.

Treat them differently than low achievers. Far too often (especially in religious or nonprofit organizations) we want to treat everyone the same, but with high achievers, that's a recipe for disaster. Christian principles teach that we respect everyone equally because we are all loved by God equally. However, that doesn't mean our gifts, talents, and skills are equal. When it comes to salaries, office hours, rules, freedom, perks, and other job-related issues, each person on the team should be rewarded based on their value to the project.

Give them the resources they need, and then get out of the way. You're only shooting yourself in the foot when you don't give high achievers the resources they need. Micromanaging is the worst thing you can do with these high performers. So don't let your insecurities as a leader get in the way of allowing them to fly.

Separate them from low achievers. Nothing will drive a high achiever crazy faster than having to work next to a low achiever. My advice? Put them on a different floor, a different room, or better yet—a different building than the other members of your team.

Pay high achievers what they're worth and stop nit-picking your best people. Sure, working for a "cause" is important, but people have to pay their bills. Obviously budgets are a challenge for everyone, but when you do have the resources, by holding back financially with your best people, you're killing a big part of their motivation. And if you don't have the budget? Look for other opportunities like time off, a more flexible schedule, etc. Rewards matter.

Finally, give them deadlines and don't be afraid to add pressure. A dirty little secret among creative people is that we actually love deadlines. The worst thing you can do is assign a project and not give your team a date when it's due. Good planning needs benchmarks.

None of these ideas needs to be overdone or cause tension in your organization. But through skillful leadership, you can take your high achievers to even higher levels, and in the process, transform your organization.

TRAINING YOUR TEAM

Here's a situation at churches and ministries I encounter from time to time: A leader with great gifts launches a church or ministry. At the start there's no money, so he or she hires friends, church members (usually young), or eager volunteers—all with very little or no experience. But the church or ministry takes off, largely because of the talent or calling of the leader.

He or she starts traveling, speaking, hosting conferences, appearing at events—all on top of preaching or teaching at the church or ministry. Things are buzzing. There are a lot of balls in the air, and the team is working day and night—almost all because of the success and/or popularity of the leader.

The problem in this scenario is that while everyone works hard and is loyal, no one on the staff has any real training on how to run or manage the growing organization. They didn't know any better at the start, because there was never an older, more experienced mentor to teach them best practices about managing an office, planning schedules, finances, HR policies, etc.

Now the team thinks they're doing it right because it's all they've ever known and they're experiencing such success. But the truth is, the success is happening only because the leader is so personally gifted, and what they're experiencing is just the tip of the iceberg of what's actually possible. Plus, if they were doing it correctly, they wouldn't be killing themselves in the process.

Then, the time comes when they reach a level where they want to expand their influence. The leader realizes it's time to publish a major book, expand their social media impact, launch a media ministry—in short, build a major platform.

But it never happens.

Expanding a leader's platform involves pesky things like focus, deadlines, commitments, scheduling, returned phone calls and e-mails, communication skills—in short, it needs to become a priority. But by now, the church or ministry is used to living moment by moment and think they have it all under control.

I asked my friend and leadership consultant Sam Chand about it. He told me, "That's the first conversation I have with my clients. It's really about responsiveness. I make it clear that I will not chase you and will drop you if I have to chase you. Also, I do not work with 'staff' alone. The CEO/lead pastor has to assume full responsibility for everything. They can't use staff for any excuses."

Sounds tough, but the truth is Sam's exactly right. To take the next steps in expanding ministry and influence, a leader has to focus and respond quickly to outside vendors, advisors, coaches, and mentors.

Is your organization like this? Do you look successful on the outside, but on the inside you're about to implode? Is your team exhausted and at the end of their rope? Are they dropping the ball? Are you experiencing rapid turnover? Inside you know you're missing opportunities, but you don't know what's wrong.

> Every organization of any size needs to understand basic management principles. They need to have a clear line of authority, employees who understand what professionalism means, and how to respond in a timely manner to people outside the organization.

What's the story on your team? Do they have the skills to take you from where you are to where you want to be? Are you on that team and recognize what I've described?

Training your team isn't always flashy, hip, or cool. But it's what creates the foundation for you to grow. We've helped teams of all kinds learn how to get in shape so I know it's not too late to start.

But the clock is ticking, and your calling matters.

DON'T BE AFRAID OF CREATIVE MISFITS

I've always been fascinated with the great artist and inventor Leonardo da Vinci, who by some accounts was a brilliant misfit. Some speculate that he may have had Asperger's, but at the very least, he didn't socialize well. Reading his biography recently reminded me of a friend who worked for a very large national nonprofit organization. She was remarkably creative, and she showed them how to use digital media in some very innovative ways. She made deals with outside firms to create apps, helped them integrate new platforms to share their message, and created a stable of young filmmakers to produce short films to help share their story.

While the donors and the public loved the new creativity, the leadership team never got it. They were set in their ways, and didn't really understand why she wanted to work late at night or weekends, challenge their policies, and dress differently than others at the organization.

In spite of the challenges, the results of her work were so successful, she finally asked her boss if she could form an official media department and be the leader. Her frustrated boss told her he'd consider it, and set up a meeting to discuss the idea. But when she arrived at the meeting, it was an ambush. Her boss had invited a guest—the head of Human Resources—who proceeded to read her the riot act about working hours, types of dress, official rules, policies to follow, and much more.

My friend was so discouraged she handed in her resignation the next morning and moved on to another job.

Since that time, the nonprofit has shrunk. Because they didn't understand the value of digital video and social media, they may eventually disappear off the radar. Plus, as their primary group of older donors has aged, they're not being replaced by younger donors—because they don't know how to speak the language of media.

The bottom line is that because they were uncomfortable with a creative misfit, they just might lose their chance at the future. Because they were set in their ways, and didn't understand how the culture has changed, they burned the bridge to the next generation.

Creative misfits shake things up. They challenge conventional thinking. They frustrate people. They don't care much about "the way we've always done it."

The lesson? Get comfortable with creative misfits, or get comfortable with struggling to survive.

STOP TAKING CREDIT FOR GREAT IDEAS

As a pastor or church leader, you're also called to be a communicator. In that role, to become truly fulfilled in your career or calling, you need to answer one important question: Which is more important: Making ideas happen, or taking credit for coming up with those ideas? I know people who pounce on every opportunity to remind people they came up with certain ideas or projects. They're willing to stop discussions, interrupt brainstorming sessions, and derail conversations, because they feel absolutely compelled to "remind" everyone: "That was my idea!"

And I understand the feeling. Any creative person wants to feel that his or her efforts are appreciated, and it never hurts when your great ideas get noticed. However—particularly as a leader—this is a problem for two reasons:

Nobody cares. At that moment, the team is interested in moving forward. They want to act on the idea, not dwell on who thought of it. It's not selfish on their part; they're just in action mode. Constant, gentle "reminders" that you thought of it first, wear other people down, and it won't take long before you and your ideas aren't welcome anymore—no matter how great they happen to be.

It also frees you. You may recall the great quote from President Ronald Reagan: "There is no limit to the amount of good you can do if you don't care who gets the credit." Not feeling a need to own all the best ideas is the essence of great leadership.

It's not about you, it's about the idea.

In fact, once you get into the habit, you'll be surprised to find that it gives you a fun little charge every time someone else takes credit for your ideas—because you allow them to feel like they came up with it.

Motivational legend Dale Carnegie believed that when you give an order to an employee or team member, they'll resent it. Maybe they won't say that to your face, but deep inside, they'll fight it because nobody likes to be ordered around. But if a person believes an idea is his, he'll fight to the death to make that idea a reality. Therefore, Carnegie's advice to leaders? Stop ordering people around, and start letting them own the idea. They'll buy into it faster and accomplish so much more.

Never be so protective of your ideas that they never actually happen.

WHY YOUR CHURCH OR MINISTRY NEEDS A R&D LAB

I was at a creative strategy meeting recently with a large nonprofit organization, and we were discussing the need to reposition the organization in the digital age. But an employee brought up an issue that had plagued them in the past. Since the beginning they'd been driven by a philosophy of "dollar in/dollar out." In other words, they felt that for every dollar spent at the ministry in whatever area—especially creative and marketing—it needs to generate a donor dollar back in.

I was about to bring up why that's a deadly philosophy for organizations when one of their leaders finally spoke up. She remarked (with a certainly amount of exasperation) that a dollar in/dollar out philosophy was what has always held them back. As a result of that thinking, they had always thought small because they couldn't possibly take the risk of new or innovative ideas that might fail. She finally pleaded that until the team was willing to take creative risks, they'll never see how far they can go, or how big they can grow.

I couldn't have said it better.

One of the ideas that helps the most successful and fast-growing churches, ministries, and nonprofits is having a virtual research and development lab within the organization. In a digital age, where technology, how we communicate, and a changing culture are transforming everything, it's more important than ever to cultivate a culture of creative experimentation. The willingness to invest time and resources into a R&D lab to constantly push the envelope makes enormous sense.

For instance, Google allows their employees 20 percent of their time to develop personal side projects; Life.Church in Oklahoma City has hosted "hack-a-thons" where they gather top computer programmers and give them a day to develop a new app to solve a problem. It's refreshing to see when so many church and ministry leaders talk about the importance of learning from failure, but never allow employees to actually experience it.

So I talked to an old friend, Rob Hoskins, who's president of one of the most innovative ministries I know—OneHope in Pompano Beach, Florida. Rob referred me to Liam Savage, OneHope's Innovation Designer. (Yes—the ministry has an "Innovation Designer" on their team.) Here's what Liam shared with me:

The first example is about our internal process. At OneHope, we formed the innovation team around the idea of a dedicated team to solve problems nobody else had the expertise to solve. We are essentially a learning team, and we come alongside other teams to help them gain clarity when operating in unfamiliar areas.

The second example is external. I'm a part of the leadership team with Indigitous, which is a network of people passionate about faith and technology. There are many different manifestations of what that looks like, everything from Christian coworking spaces as entrepreneurship and outreach, to developing digital evangelism strategies, to theology for Silicon Valley. Everyone who joins has a slightly different approach, but it all centers on helping the church meaningfully engage with technology.

YouVersion is also taking part. Indigitous hosts a global hackathon every year, and I believe we've had over eighty cities participate over the past three years. These events are usually hosted by churches, university students, Christian business owners or nonprofits who invite a broader audience of coders and designers and each location produces several solutions to the challenges issued by the host organization, the community, or the global challenges we face.

Internal and external—both ways OneHope has created opportunities to experiment and innovate.

Whatever situation you're in— how could you empower your team to experiment?

It may be with a local evangelism campaign, internal communication, evaluating projects, volunteer training, media—any number of areas could benefit from this kind of free-flowing, no pressure experimentation.

Dawn Nicole Baldwin, who leads our communication and growth strategies at Cooke Media Group, offered a good reason so many churches and ministries fail to innovate like OneHope is doing:

What holds many organizations back is simply being afraid of failure (because others are watching). We think we don't have enough resources to do it, but in reality our challenges with time, people, or money are more often our mindset. Plus, it's not just leaders who don't allow employees to experiment. Oftentimes it's the congregation, elders, board, and others who make it hard for the leader. The bottom line is that if the marketplace feels innovation is important for something as trivial as laundry detergent, shouldn't we experiment when so much more is at stake?

WHEN CREATIVE LEADERS BECOME INSTITUTIONALIZED

From media production to communication strategy to coaching through a crisis, I love creative teams focused on helping organizations share their message with the culture. But when organizations stop innovating, they start dying. Time to time, I encounter leaders who have become institutionalized. They play it safe, stop taking risks, and look for the easy way out.

The truth is, nobody starts out to be average. So the question becomes, how did they get that way?

In these situations I'm reminded of the revealing quote by the prison inmate "Red" played by Morgan Freeman, when he described his older friend "Brooks" in the movie "Shawshank Redemption." When asked why Brooks didn't want to leave the prison, even though his sentence was served, Red replied:

"First, you hate the walls, then you get used to them, then you depend on them."

At first, creative leaders hate average. They push the boundaries and really want to make a difference in the culture. They're willing to put in the hours, take the criticism, and fight for what they believe in.

But after a time, they get tired of the long hours, the critical clients or coworkers, church members, investors, or donors who don't get it. They ease up, thinking that it just takes time, so why push it? After all, those who are pushing back are also our supporters or employers, so let's not upset them. We'll give it some time and people will change. It's perfectly understandable.

But after a few years of easing up, they get used to the regular hours, the support of influential people, and never having to defend their ideas. After all, it's easier, so why rock the boat? So pastors or CEO's enjoy the support of the board. Creatives leave the freelance life and take a full-time job. Leaders stop pushing their team.

And before long, they depend on the walls. If they're honest, they'll admit that they look fondly back on the old creative days, but realize now it was just a youthful dream, and now they understand that creativity, business, or ministry is serious. So they work within the system. They lie to themselves.

Fortunately, some realize their mistake and break out of the walls. Not many do that because it's tough—very tough. But for most, living inside the walls works. It's easier to go unchallenged, have a nice office, and keep the respect of those who love the way things have always been done.

So—pastor, ministry leader, communications person, filmmaker, creative type—whatever you are, the question is—where are you now? At what point did you get bought off with a raise, a new title, or better office? At what point did you give up?

And perhaps more important, what are you willing to sacrifice to break out of those walls?

THERE MAY BE A BETTER ALTERNATIVE TO HIRING FULL-TIME EMPLOYEES

As churches and ministries grow, most pastors and leaders are convinced they need to hire more full-time employees. Perhaps it's the security of having the team around all the time, or maybe it's a loyalty issue, or perhaps it's the mistaken idea that to understand the DNA of an organization you have to be there full time. Whatever it is, thinking only in terms of full-time employees hurts the organization and can actually hold it back.

> The truth is, you can often get far more qualified people
> by engaging freelancers or consultants
> than you can by hiring full time.

Most freelancers and consultants have that job for a reason—they're good enough and have risen to a professional level that multiple organizations want them, so they have the opportunity to impact more than one team.

Plus, in many positions, you don't really need a full-time employee as much as you think. For instance, do you really need a full-time person in areas like:

Graphic design?

Video production?

Video post-production?

Social media?

Website development?

Writing?

Donor development?

Audio production?

Lighting?

I could go on and on, but you get the picture.

Pastors and leaders—start thinking more in terms of how temporary or part-time employees could bring an entirely new level of expertise to your situation. Why pay full-time benefits and salaries for what could be a short-term need?

Freelancers or consultants just might be your answer.

DON'T DELEGATE TO SOMEONE WHO UNDERMINES YOU

In most cases, when an organization hires my company, they name someone internally as the "point person" who we work with on a day-to-day basis. In some cases, this point person has approval authority, and at the very least dictates the working relationship. In most cases, the person is experienced, responsible, and qualified. But from time to time, the wrong point person can make life miserable.

In the last twenty years, here are some of the "point people" who have evaluated and critiqued our work for clients:

-> *A housewife (she was a friend of the pastor and had worked in marketing ten years ago).*

-> *The CEO's assistant, right out of college (because he had taken a film class).*

-> *The ministry's youth director (after all, teens like videos, right?).*

-> *The CEO's cousin (because she had a "good design sense").*

-> *A church member who'd recently finished an anger management course (because he wanted to be a filmmaker one day).*

In the most cases, it's an employee who simply doesn't care. They have other work to do, or believe this project isn't a priority, so they put it in their "someday" box. They take forever to return phone calls, review the work, or communicate with anyone, which also makes it look like we're not meeting deadlines.

I could go on, but you get the point. In each case, these people were approving and changing work done by far more experienced and qualified designers, video producers, writers, and other creatives.

In each case it was a disaster.

> **You've probably gone to a lot of effort to find the right outside designer, video producer, branding consultant, writer, and others to help tell your story. Plus, you're probably paying them a lot of money for their talent. So don't undermine that effort by assigning an unqualified employee to be your point person on the project.**

Fortunately, the vast majority of our team's work is directly with senior leadership, so that ability to report directly eliminates an enormous amount of frustration or confusion. In other cases, my recommendation is that the leader who initiates the project be involved in the beginning to set the vision and set checkpoints along the way.

TEN VITAL KEYS ABOUT DESIGNING A CREATIVE CULTURE

It's no secret that culture is more important than vision. I've worked in creative, vibrant cultures where original thinking is valued and wonderful things happen. On the other hand I've worked at organizations where you could literally feel the oppression when you walked into the building. Those destructive cultures often have leaders with great vision and potential, but because the culture is so negative, that vision will never be realized.

How do you create a creative culture? Here are ten principles I've used to turn around numerous organizational cultures:

1. Creative people need stability. If they're worried about losing their job, financial problems, or excessive turnover, they'll never release their best ideas. I've seen terrible leaders think they're motivating the team by threatening them with being fired—which is the worst thing you could ever do. Even when you're going through difficult times, create an atmosphere of stability for the team. You'll be rewarded down the road.

2. Make it safe from excessive criticism. Critics are a dime a dozen, but leaders who can help their team move from bad ideas to legendary ideas are rare. There's a time to look at what doesn't work, but that should be done in an atmosphere of trust. Criticism always goes down better when it comes from a trusted and respected source.

3. Make sure your leaders are on the same page. All it takes is one of your leaders to contradict what you're trying to do to wreck a creative culture. At the beginning of building your culture, make absolutely sure your leadership team is unified and moving with you. One critical or disconnected leader or manager can sow seeds of doubt that will topple the entire project.

4. Be flexible. Creative people don't all operate on the same schedule or work the same way. Give your team some flexibility and it will revolutionize their attitude. At one major organization I talked the CEO into allowing the creative team to rip up carpet, repaint, dump the cubicles, and design their own work spaces. There was fear and trembling on the CEO's part, but within a matter of months, the creative team transformed the ministry.

5. Get them the tools they need. Nothing drags a creative team down as much as broken, old, or out-of-date tools. Sure we all have budget challenges, but do whatever you can to get them the right computers, design tools, video equipment—and whatever else they need. Think about it: The less time and energy they spend overcoming technical and equipment problems, the more time and energy they can spend on developing amazing ideas.

6. Push them outside their comfort zone. Leaders often think that creative people want to be left alone and operate on their own schedule. Sure they like to create their own timetable, but they also relish a challenge. In fact, while they probably won't admit it, creative people love deadlines because it gives them perspective on the project. I don't even start working until I can see the deadline approaching. There is just something about a challenge that gets my blood flowing and the ideas coming.

7. Get out of their way. One of the most important aspects of a creative culture, once it's in process, is to get out of the way of your creative team. We all know micromanaging is a disaster for anyone—especially creatives. So give them space and let them solve problems on their own.

8. Understand the difference between *organizational* structure and *communication* structure. This is a huge issue for me. Every organization needs an organizational structure. Who reports to who matters, and hierarchy is important. But when it comes to communication, I recommend you throw the organizational structure out the window. Your creative team should be able to call anyone to ask questions and discuss ideas. Don't force them to communicate through supervisors, managers, or anyone else. Create a free-flowing communication system, and the ideas will grow.

9. Walk the factory floor. Leadership expert John Maxwell recommends that leaders "walk the factory floor" and meet every employee. Develop a personal relationship with employees at all levels—especially when it comes to your creative team. Former Pixar and Disney Animation President Ed Catmull takes that seriously—even when it comes to giving bonuses. When they produce a box-office success, they share the profits with the team that produced it—which often numbers more than one hundred people. But Ed doesn't just mail or direct deposit the check and send a nice note. Ed takes the time to either go to each team member personally or invite them to his office individually and hand them the check—and tell them how much their work is appreciated.

10. **Give them credit.** Finally, a great creative culture allows everyone to be noticed for their accomplishments. Never take credit for your team's work, and always give them the honor that's due. You'll find that when you protect your creative team and allow them to get the glory for their work, they'll follow you into a fire.

KEY PRINCIPLES TO CONSIDER ABOUT LEADING CREATIVE PEOPLE:

1. **To be successful in today's ministry world, having a creative team around you is critical.**

2. **Of all your tasks as a leader, developing your team is one of the most important.** Taking the time every day to teach, encourage, and inspire your team will reap more benefits than you can possibly imagine.

3. **Culture is more important than vision.** You can have the greatest vision for your ministry in the world, but if you haven't created a culture within your organization that can make that vision happen, you'll fail.

4. **Spend time training your team.** You can't expect them to perform at a high level without proper training. Every organization of any size needs to understand basic management principles. They need to have a clear line of authority, employees who understand what professionalism means, and how to respond in a timely manner to people outside the organization.

5. **Develop a "Research and Development" department in your church or ministry.** This doesn't have to be a big-budget operation, because

it starts with your organization's culture. Give them the latitude to try, fail, and try again. You'll discover amazing new options and revitalize your team in the process.

6. **Don't hinder your relationship with outside consultants or vendors by putting an unprepared or inexperienced employee as the point-person in the relationship.** Depending on the level of the outside expert, chances are, they need direct access to the top leader.

— 5 —

LEAD BETTER MEETINGS

"If you had to identify, in one word, the reason why the human race has not achieved, and never will achieve, its full potential, that word would be 'meetings.'"

—Dave Barry

Why talk about meetings in a book about communication and media? Simple. Communication and media are team sports. Getting everyone on the same page to accomplish your goals is a priority, and that usually happens around meetings.

As the leader, in most cases you'll be in charge of your meetings. Much of this chapter is really written to help you manage others in the room. So read it, but perhaps more important is that you teach these principles to your team. When everyone is on the same page, meeting can become fuel that helps propel creative ideas forward.

I've written a lot about meetings over the years, mostly because I just hate them. The vast majority are wasteful, unproductive, and distract employees from the actual task of getting things done. But no matter how much I (and plenty of others) write about the evils of meetings, organizations still have them. Now, I've finally discovered why:

> In bureaucratic organizations, far too many employees think the *process* is the goal. They think that policies, meetings, and paperwork is their job—when these areas are only tools to get the job done.

These employees schedule meetings on the mistaken premise that the meeting is the task itself. In my mind, very few things could be more damaging to a company. As a result, full-time employees in big organizations schedule endless meetings, create shelves of policies, and talk about work instead of actually *doing* work.

I understand that sometimes we need meetings. People do need to be on the same page, and a productive meeting can be enormously helpful. But for all the others, I'm calling for a boycott. Be tough. Be the obstinate person in your organization willing to stand up to the meeting bullies. Remind them that meetings usually hurt more than help. Remind them that policies may be important, but they're not the reason your organization exists.

Stop talking and start doing. Take it to the streets and don't back down. Maybe it's time to start a "no meetings revolution."

MY RULES FOR ATTENDING MEETINGS

OK, that's not a real solution, and I get it. But if I have to attend a meeting, I want it to be productive. Over the years I've actually fired employees who couldn't control themselves during meetings (I'll explain later). If you're on my team and attending a client meeting, branding meeting, production meeting, or any other kind of meeting with me, you have to know what I expect. Here's a list of things I want my people to know during a meeting, and the list might be worth sharing with your team as well:

Listen. Nothing is more important in a meeting than simply listening. Too many people in meetings aren't really listening, they're just thinking of the next thing to say. That never works, because if you haven't been listening, whatever you say will be wrong or inappropriate.

One of the people I fired couldn't keep his mouth shut during client meetings. He was a brand-new employee and knew nothing about the client or problem we were discussing. But he kept interrupting the meeting with his ideas—none of which were relevant to the problem. Over and over I asked him to control himself, but he simply couldn't help it. So I had to let him go.

If an idea pops into your head during a meeting, write it down first. Never blurt out that brilliant revelation you just received. Jot it down first, and then see when it would be appropriate to interject it into the conversation. Far too often, the idea that just hit you isn't what we're actually discussing at the moment. (Plus, writing it down gives you a minute to decide if it's worth sharing at all and could save you from embarrassment.)

Don't tell us about your life story, the dream project you're working on, or some new insight you recently read about. Above all, don't preach. Honor the people in the room and focus on the task at hand. You don't need to subtly remind us that you're an important part of the meeting.

Do your homework. Nothing is more embarrassing than tossing out an idea that's already been tried or already failed. Learn about the client or project before walking in the room. And if you don't know, then lean over and whisper it to a colleague first. Make sure that what you contribute is something new and worth their time. Never walk into a meeting blind.

Stop interrupting! Nothing anyone has to say is so important that it's worth interrupting. Just bide your time, and speak when it's appropriate. When you interrupt someone, you're telling everyone in the meeting that his or her comment isn't worth listening to and that you're much more important.

Finally, never dominate the meeting. Keep your comments short and to the point. As you talk, watch the reactions of other people in the room. Are they listening? Are they interested? Or have they tuned you out? Cut to the chase. As my pastor father once described "popcorn testimonies" in church: "Pop up, pop off, then pop right back down." That's good advice for meetings.

ADVOCACY VERSUS INQUIRY AND THE KEY TO SUCCESSFUL MEETINGS

How many of your meetings involve advocacy versus inquiry? That's really just a fancy way of asking if the discussions in your meetings are about *defending people's ideas*, or about *asking honest questions*. Far too many employees spend most of their time defending themselves and not nearly enough time listening and being open to new ideas.

You can't win with advocacy because everyone spends their time trying to prove they are right. The kind of advocacy I'm talking about is driven by insecurity and causes people to focus on being right more than making a difference.

Meetings driven by honest inquiry on the other hand open the door to new ideas, innovation, and original thinking. If the best ideas don't win in your meetings, then it's time to change how you approach the discussion.

MEETING DISRUPTORS

I attend a lot of meetings, and although 90 percent of them are unnecessary, I realize the remaining few can be incredibly important. Pitching an idea, making a presentation, networking, coaching, leading a team, getting project updates, and more, usually need meetings in order to happen. But in far too many cases, most of us would admit to massive meeting failure. The big project doesn't happen, your creative idea is turned down, you're outvoted, or the presentation goes south.

So what's the problem? Over the last year or two, I've been making notes on why meetings go bad, and I've discovered seven kinds of people who most commonly disrupt meetings. Take a hard look at this list, because chances are, one or more of these people may be on your team and keeping you from being more successful at your meetings.

The person who won't stop talking. I was invited to coffee last year by a guy pitching his company's services to our team. But from the moment we sat down, he launched into a nonstop pitch about himself, his company, his product, his past, all the people he knew, and more. Never once did he ask about us, our company, or what we need. It was a one-way monologue, and one that I'll never be part of again.

The person who checks his mobile device. Last spring I was in a meeting with two people, and each time one talked to me, the other pulled out his iPhone and checked his messages. That instantly telegraphed to me that his phone was more important than our meeting. I finally said, "Why don't you respond to your messages and then we'll continue the meeting." Even after that, he kept checking! I won't be meeting with him again.

The person who doesn't prepare. At a meeting recently, a woman (who called the meeting) asked me, "I really don't know anything about you. What do you actually do?" A brief five-minute glance at my blog or our company website would have told her 95 percent of what she needed, but she obviously hadn't even taken the time to do that.

The person who is late. Showing up late for a meeting tells me that you don't value my time. Enough said.

The person who won't get to the point. There's a lady I've now had two meetings with and I honestly can't tell you what she does or what she wants. Trust me, there won't be a third meeting. (I'm amazed I gave her two.) Get to the point. Make it simple to understand. Don't waste people's time.

The person who isn't dressed appropriately or eats by himself during the meeting. I'm a casual guy and will give people a lot of grace when it comes to personal appearance. But never forget that the way you dress, along with your overall attitude, is communicating a message. I've also been in meetings where the leader sat down to a complete breakfast (eggs, bacon, toast) as two assistants served him. While he was enjoying himself immensely, he never offered anything to the other people in the room.

Finally, the person who doesn't care about me. I can usually tell within a few minutes if the other person cares about me or is only interested in what I can do for him or her. You'll get far more from relationships if the relationship is more important than what you want out of it. The old saying is true: People don't care how much you know until they know how much you care.

HOW TO BEHAVE IN OTHER PEOPLE'S MEETINGS

I'm often invited (and honored) to observe other organization's meetings. For instance, a few years ago in South Africa, my friend, Pastor Alan Platt, invited Kathleen and me to observe a meeting of church and ministry leaders from fifty countries who were planning *Movement Day,* the goal of which is to catalyze leadership teams from the world's largest cities. It would be a major event, learning how to serve their cities more effectively by advancing high-level, city-changing partnerships. In essence, they were planning workshop tracks, themes, and other issues. Sitting through that experience reminded me of how people should act and respond when invited to meetings that don't directly involve them.

It wasn't my meeting so I held back. I was honored to be invited, and I knew I was there to observe, not necessarily contribute. In the case of my South Africa meeting, I learned that the event had been in the planning stages for more than three years. Many of the leaders in the room had been working online together for a year, and the meeting I observed was the end of a week of hard, collaborative work. Even though I felt I had ideas to contribute, it would be enormous hubris to assume I had some "revelation" they hadn't thought of in the last three years. My one hour of experience with the issue was enough to keep me quiet in the presence of their previous three years of work.

I also recognized it was better to practice discernment when you're in a group with which you're unfamiliar. In my case, I didn't immediately know their theological perspective, experience planning events like this, or the identity or background of everyone at the table. Speaking too soon—even when invited—can be a recipe for disaster.

I did make lots of notes. If you do feel that you can contribute, or see mistakes being made, talk about it privately with whoever invited you to the meeting. Those in the meeting don't know you, haven't developed a trust relationship with you, and have no idea of what you may bring to the table. Respect their investment, and rather than interrupt or blurt out something to the group, mention it privately to a colleague who can vet your ideas appropriately—then decide whether or not to share with the larger group.

The higher you go in your career, the more opportunities you'll have to observe important and strategic meetings. These meetings will open your mind to amazing opportunities, introduce you to world changers, and give you new perspectives on your future. Take the humble route.

Honoring those at the table, and holding your contributions until appropriate, will be an important step in being invited to the next one.

STOP MEETING IN CONFERENCE ROOMS

Now let's go one step further—stop having meetings in the conference room and start meeting at the place where the problem lives. Meeting at the location of the problem allows everyone to see it, point to it, and discuss specifics.

That's why I'm a big advocate of meeting at the spot where the problem lies. That may be the sanctuary, a video studio, parking lot, or other location. Look at it, discuss it, find a solution, and then move on. Then step back and see how much your productivity increases.

THE ELEPHANTS IN THE ROOM

Too many organizations have areas that "just aren't discussed," so the question should be asked: What "un-discussable" subjects haunt the meetings at your organization? What are the issues that no one has the courage to bring up? What are the elephants in the room that everyone refuses to point out?

In one church it was the hiring of a pastor's friend who had no experience whatsoever. But because he had little self-awareness, he would make major pronouncements in meetings that everyone else knew were ridiculous.

At a large ministry, it was a donor development executive who was obviously failing, but she was brilliant at "managing up" so the leader refused to address the dramatic drop in donations.

Large, influential organizations are often crippled by limited thinking, and the refusal to broach certain issues. Sometimes it's the fear of losing power or respect, sometimes it's insecurity, sometimes it's ego, and sometimes it's the concern of losing a job. But whatever it is, the organization, the mission, and you suffer.

Think about it. Have courage. Push the button. Point out the elephant. Start the conversation that pulls back the curtain and exposes the real problem. Because until that happens, nothing will ever change.

A MEETING WITH TOTAL HONESTY

A remarkable thing happened to me the other day. I was in a client meeting, and the CEO opened the meeting with a statement that surprised me. He said, "This is a very important meeting about the future of our media strategy. That's why I need everyone here to be absolutely honest. I know we have problems, and we're looking for solutions. You are protected here. Whatever you say will not impact your job in a negative way whatsoever. I'm looking for real answers, and I need you to be completely honest and accurate." Then he opened it up for discussion.

That request totally changed the dynamic of the meeting.

Everyone knew he was serious, and that he actually meant what he said. When he finished, it was like pulling the curtain back to reveal the unvarnished truth about the organization. People were honest—but not cruel or vindictive. They respected each other, but the new atmosphere allowed everyone in the room to let go and be comfortable saying things they might ordinarily have held back.

As a result, we started some dramatic changes within the organization. Positive changes that will have a great impact on the future. What did that experience teach me?

It takes courage to start up a meeting like that. You never know what people might say, and I admired the leader for opening up to possible criticism. Many leaders I know don't want to hear that kind of honesty from their own people.

It needs to happen more often. I sit in too many meetings where the truth is thrown under the bus. Politics prevail, and kingdoms continue to be built. It does nothing but muck up the works, and make real success harder to come by.

It's not about getting even, it's about fixing problems. Be gracious, because you rarely know all the circumstances from your position around the table.

Commit to a life of "brutal honesty." Being honest doesn't mean being ugly or mean; it's about speaking the truth in confidence, and with the expertise to back it up.

Let's all decide to have more meetings like this one.

KEY PRINCIPLES TO CONSIDER ABOUT LEADING MEETINGS:

1. **Never start a meeting without an agenda.** Always have a purpose and write out the goals ahead of the meeting.

2. **Have a predetermined stop time for the meeting.** People should know when it will be over so they can plan the rest of their day.

3. **Consider moving your meetings to where the problem lives.** It can be far more efficient when you meet where the problem is happening. A visual reference can spark much better ideas and solutions.

4. **Meetings are not the *goal*, they're the *process*.** Meetings are the catalyst, not the end purpose.

5. **Lead meetings, don't just participate.** Don't let your meetings (or attendees) wander. Keep them on point.

6. **Experiment with your meetings.** Try shorter meetings, stand-up meetings, walking meetings, smaller meetings, and more. Getting stuck in a "meeting rut" is the best way to kill creative ideas.

— 6 —

MARKETING, COMMUNICATION, AND YOUR WEBSITE

"Marketing is really just about sharing your passion."

—Michael Hyatt

Mastering media starts with knowing what each platform does best. Too many leaders use media randomly, with no real strategic vision. Perhaps a friend recommended local TV, or a board member suggested billboards, or a church youth director likes social media. All these platforms and others are important, but the question is: Why? While I could write many books on the subject, here's a short list of what differentiates some of the major media platforms:

Newspaper Advertising:
- –> While traditional newspapers are disappearing across the country, they still exist in many cities and towns and can be an effective way to reach 50+ adults since they are the primary readers of newspapers.
- –> Newspapers are by definition a local media tool and can provide opportunities to create "newsworthiness."
- –> Newspapers are good for more in-depth stories.

TV:

–> Research indicates the typical household watches 8+ hours of TV daily.

–> TV still delivers the largest audiences for specific programming.

–> Blockbuster movies get more publicity, but the truth is, a popular TV series reaches far more people.

–> The growing number of special interest TV channels provides opportunities to target specific audiences and leverage their interests.

Radio:

–> Despite what you might think while listening to Christian radio, music is still the top reason that people tune in to radio.

–> Drive time is still important. 78 percent of consumers listen to the radio on their drive to work.

–> Similar to TV, specific radio formats appeal to different segments (young, old, multicultural, faith, etc.)

Outdoor Advertising:

–> Billboards and other outdoor advertising can be a powerful local tool.

–> It can be very effective for promoting local churches.

–> It reaches a broad range of different target audiences and provides local geographic flexibility.

–> The recent growth of billboards has revealed new outdoor advertising products like digital video or LED screens that reach and engage consumers throughout the day.

–> New media tactics like gas station advertising, stadium advertising, and health club advertising are examples of highly targeted media products that reach and engage consumers.

Internet / Digital / Social Media:

–> Digital advertising is still innovating as marketers look for the right mix that provides meaningful information and will attract consumers to a website.

-> Similar to other media choices, consumers have the ability to opt-in and choose what digital advertising they see and consume.

-> For churches, virtually 100 percent of new visitors will check you out online first.

-> Your website is your "media hub." It can be the connector to your video, bookstore resources, social media pages, and much more.

-> The 55+ audience watches as many online videos as the 20+ audience.

-> Significant numbers of online viewers of videos want to find out more about the subject of the video.

-> With social media platforms, you can start with a zero budget. It literally takes nothing to build a tribe and start sharing your message with significant numbers of people.

There are many more strengths to each of these platforms, as well as other powerful marketing and advertising tools you haven't even considered. Before you get in a rut, find out as much as possible about new platforms and consider how they could help your message reach a greater and more responsive audience.

LEARN HOW PEOPLE COMMUNICATE

When it comes to communication, let's begin with the world you operate in every day—connecting effectively with your family, employees, board members, and others close to you is vital to making your calling happen. From that perspective, two major types of communicators you need to understand are people who think by talking, and people who think by doing. I'm a doer. Maybe it's my short attention span, but I'm really not interested in most details.

A former team member at our media production and strategy company Cooke Media Group was a detail guy. That's a big reason I brought him on the team. He had a white board in his office with circles, arrows, buzzwords, and other stuff—it was just filled. He wanted to look under the hood of projects and rummage around in there. I just want to see the dashboard: Tell me how fast we're going, and if we have enough gas, and I'm fine.

**Which communication style is your board?
Your biggest donors? Influential advisors?
The people you regularly communicate with?**

When my team brings me detailed reports, or ramble on and on, I mentally check out. When overly detailed people schedule an appointment with me, my assistant tells them "When his eyes glaze over, the meeting is done." If you want to get to me, it's bullet points, not details.

**The point is? We are constantly frustrated
because we don't take the time to learn how
people communicate—and we don't teach
our team how to communicate with us.**

It's not about "better or worse." Both styles work, but are very different—and you'll never accomplish much if you don't learn and respond to the ways different people communicate. Know who you're talking to, and make sure the message you transmit is the message that's received. Likewise, don't assume your team understands how to communicate with you. Sometimes, we need to take the time to make it clear.

THE IMPORTANCE OF BUILDING A COMMUNICATION TEAM

Recently I received an e-mail from a friend who was let go from a major nonprofit organization who had slashed their communication department. I had to put that e-mail in the growing folder I'd received over the last year from others in similar situations. It seems that whenever a church, ministry, or nonprofit gets into financial difficulty, the first department to eliminate is communication. After all, do we really need that social media or video person? Surely we can trim our designer, right?

Here's the problem with that kind of thinking: The job of your communication team is to multiply your message.

That sermon you preach, the fundraising appeal, your missions outreach, the homeless shelter you build, or the meals you provide—it's their job to take that message to the world. Which means that without your communication team, your message, and by extension your impact will be diminished and possibly eliminated. You would be surprised to know the number of calls I've taken from leaders in desperation who say that a few years earlier, they eliminated their communication department, stopped using TV or radio to share their message, or terminated other media campaigns because budgets were tight.

But now, they realize it was a huge mistake.

After months or years, they now understand that decision meant they cut ties with donors and supporters—not to mention losing the ability to share their message with the general public. They call because they want to relaunch their communication and media effort. But by then it's like starting all over. The donors have moved on, social media followers changed their allegiance, and media viewers and listeners are now interested in something else.

In a media-driven culture, it's time to stop thinking that communication or media is expendable.

Of course your teaching, evangelism, missions, education, and other work is paramount. It's the reason you exist. But if you're not telling that story well, then your effort—and your impact—will be limited. In today's media-driven culture, no matter how great your work and message, if no one knows about it, you've failed. Maybe it's time to rethink your priorities when it comes to communication and media, and our next section is knowing where to start.

NO-BUDGET MARKETING AND PROMOTION

But where do you start when you don't have a media or communication budget? In the traditional sense, marketing takes money. Print ads, billboards, radio and TV spots aren't cheap. But most of my clients don't have that kind of money, and most aren't very influential (yet) in their field. From a traditional publicity standpoint, that's a death knell. But not in the digital age. Today, no matter what your budget, I recommend working the grassroots—from the bottom up. Here are some examples of what I mean:

Make your advertising or promotions easy to find. Particularly when it comes to video promotion, start with the easy routes and upload them to YouTube and social media platforms. Even producing amateur videos is a start. Then do your best to get them on the specific sites that are important to your church or ministry.

Use your own networks. All your leaders should use their own personal networks, and e-mail a personal note to their relationships telling them about the event/project/program and send them a link. (It's helpful when the link goes to a branded page from your church or ministry with the video, or other promotional information.) Never forget that people prefer to follow other people (more than organizations) so your team's *personal* networks are vitally important.

Fire up the blogosphere. Contact all the influential bloggers in your area of expertise or interest and ask them to comment or review your project on their blogs. When people see the buzz on the blogs, influencers will start to notice.

Work the blogs from the backend. Have your staff or interns scour online blogs for appropriate discussions, and then participate, using your project/event/advertising as an example. For instance, they could respond to a post with: "I completely agree that technology will never overpower storytelling, and here's a great example: (insert link)." Don't have them do it as your employees, just regular web surfers. You can get an amazing number of conversations going on a variety of issues, using your work or outreaches as examples.

Who are the influencers? Publishers send advance copies of books to the influencers in the appropriate industry or topic area to promote upcoming books, and you should do the same with your work. Whether they act on it or not, it helps keep you on the radar with the people that matter.

Finally, brief your financial person or fundraising team about the campaign. I'm sure they would have special relationships or potential donors they could show the material to who would be responsive.

> ## The key is that in the digital media world, we can't control publicity solely from a top-down direction anymore.

People want a conversation about events, products, and ideas, so we have to learn how *they* want to communicate. Using social media and blogs are good ways to start that conversation—especially if we can define exactly what you're promoting can mean for them. I would encourage you to create a story around the project. What does it mean for the future of causes like this? Is this a new type of outreach or strategy? Whatever it might be (and make the niche as tight as possible), it will give you a platform and a bigger reason to talk about it—and more important—for other people to talk about it.

Finally, for you or members of your team to speak on current issues at outside events and conferences is incredibly helpful in terms of your perception. It's not just about you as the boss. In the most effective churches and ministries, team members like the youth director, missions director, graphic designer, or social media person is recognized as a leader in that world. Think of the impact if your entire leadership team was recognized by the outside world for their expertise. You can't measure the influence that could have in your public perception.

SHOULD YOUR WORSHIP LEADER ALSO LEAD COMMUNICATION?

In many churches, the worship leader is also the leader of the communication or media team. After all, it can make sense—a good worship leader knows music, knows how to communicate a message, understands the experience of being onstage, and has the trust of the pastor. Especially in a small church it's a logical choice. But as a church grows, it could lead to challenges, and here's why:

A worship leader is a worship leader first. He or she will always look at everything through those eyes, consider the worship department and team a priority, and no matter how mature, naturally slant decisions in that direction.

Great worship is important, but is only a part of the overall outreach of the church. A communication or media director needs to understand balance in a church's message. For instance, while the new worship album is terrific, its promotion needs to be integrated into the overall messaging and branding of the church.

Invariably, where worship leaders are media directors, I've noticed that camera placement, lighting, staging are all designed around the worship set, and not the pastor's message. Again, a strong media director needs to understand the balance.

In the same way, when worship leaders also lead communication, I've noticed the equipment related to music is always amazing, while the equipment related to video, live streaming, and other communication areas is often neglected, or less expensive and effective. It's often the same way when it comes to the salary and experience levels of each team.

This is in no way meant to disparage great worship leaders, and I have no doubt that in some cases it can work. But the bottom line is *balance*. A communication strategy involves sharing the message and brand identity of the church without undue influence from any single department. While there are remarkably capable, seasoned, and mature worship leaders in churches today, leading worship and music well is a full-time responsibility in itself. Therefore, let's allow them to focus on worship and music and be amazing.

Adding communication and media under that authority is far too often viewed as an "add-on" and not given the weight and responsibility it deserves.

FIVE FAST LAUNCH TIPS FOR A NEW LOGO, NAME, OR PROJECT

We've seen it happen too often. Significant time, energy, and dollars are invested in the creation of a new name, logo, or project, with little consideration dedicated to what happens next. Just a few years ago, a major ministry organization changed their name. The reason for the change was good, but they rolled it out so poorly, it seriously damaged their brand and national perception. And sadly, that case isn't unusual at all.

Whether it's a new name, logo, ministry, or location, HOW something is rolled out is just as important as WHAT is being rolled out. With this in mind, I asked Dawn Nicole Baldwin, our lead strategist at Cooke Media Group, to highlight five of the most important things to be thinking about when planning your next launch. Here are her recommendations:

Consider your audience—Who needs to know what and when? The timing and amount of information should align with how close someone is to the heart of your ministry. Those closest to the heart of the organization should get more details sooner than those on the fringes. Be intentional about mapping out what information is shared when and to whom to help equip your advocates to answer questions within their circles of influence.

This is an All-Skate—What facility needs should we consider for celebrations and interim team meetings? What budgets are we working within? Are we creating a street team to get the word out, or do we need volunteers at the event itself? What is the messaging and campaign theme? What is the overall goal and how are we defining the launch as a success? Involving multiple departments in the planning from the beginning helps to answer these questions, as well as a host of others when voices from operations, serving/connection team leaders, communications, and senior leadership are at the table early on. This cross-pollination of thinking can help your launch to be more successful by ensuring your bases are covered and can avoid last-minute surprises.

Allow time to build momentum—A faucet is a great visual for this. At least a month out, start dripping content slowly, increase the "volume" leading up to launch, and turn on full blast right before and during launch. In a busy and distracted world, people are just beginning to hear your message at the point you're sick of talking about it. Be sure to allow enough time for people to get excited and get others involved.

Include action steps—What do we want people to DO? It's not enough to just tell people something is changing. Think about what we want them to do with this information. Is it to invite a friend to the launch party? Tag someone on social media? Join the street team to help get the word out? Provide a simple, clear, next step to increase engagement and don't overwhelm them with options.

Don't slam on the brakes—Despite all the planning, there are still people who are going to miss the big reveal. Be sure to continue your communication push in the days (and weeks) that follow, slowly turning that communication faucet back off.

THE POWER OF A GREAT TAGLINE

Churches and ministries often use taglines, but don't really understand their power. A powerful tagline can help explain your brand, and more importantly, they can inspire people to act. While producing a documentary film in India on the impact of legendary missionary William Carey, I was reminded of the power of a creative tagline. Carey, who many consider the father of the modern missionary movement, organized a missionary society in 1792 and launched an evangelistic meeting with the line:

"Expect great things from God;
attempt great things for God."

That line so inspired the people of his time that in spite of widespread skepticism of missions, within a year, he was on a ship traveling to India to begin his ministry. The book *131 Christians Everyone Should Know* by the editors of *Christian History* magazine, describes the influence of that simple but powerful line:

> His greatest legacy was in the worldwide missionary movement of the nineteenth century that he inspired. Missionaries like Adoniram Judson, Hudson Taylor, and David Livingstone, among thousands of others, were impressed not only by Carey's example, but by his words: "Expect great things; attempt great things." The history of nineteenth-century Protestant missions is in many ways an extended commentary on the phrase.

When it comes to corporations, you can go all the way back to "The Pause That Refreshes" (Coca-Cola 1927). When used well, taglines have made a dramatic difference in capturing the attention of consumers with a well-crafted statement.

The next time you need a great line to launch a product, sermon series, fundraising campaign, or to change your perception in the community, remember missionary William Carey. He started his career as a businessman making shoes, and didn't have any training in advertising. And yet his one single line inspired one of the greatest missionary movements in history.

Will your next tagline have that much power?

BE CAREFUL USING GIMMICKS TO MARKET YOUR MESSAGE

I can't leave this section without saying a cautionary word about using gimmicks in our marketing and communication. The dictionary defines "gimmick" as: *"An ingenious or novel device, scheme or stratagem, especially one designed to attract attention or increase appeal."*

This may sound strange, but one of the biggest reasons I work in media ministry today is that growing up, I thought pastors were so embarrassing. Being a preacher's kid in the South during the 50s and 60s was tough, and a big reason was that pastors were always doing wacky stuff to attract attention. I recall one pastor who sat perched on a chair atop a two-story-high pole until Sunday attendance hit a certain number. Another one locked himself in the steeple, praying for revival. You may remember youth directors who shaved their head if the kids brought enough visitors. Witnessing to a friend at school was much more difficult when his big question was, "Why does Pastor Jones do such stupid things?"

From an early age I was incredibly sensitive to church gimmicks and the thinking that outrageous stunts would help reach more people with the Gospel. Don't get me wrong. Most of those leaders were incredibly sincere; they genuinely wanted to expand the Kingdom. Unfortunately, they didn't realize what the most creative communicators know:

Gimmicks may get attention, but truly original ideas change the world.

Today, I'm seeing another wave of gimmicks from a new generation of leaders—outrageous billboards, sex and technology-related stunts, mock events in their community—all to get attention and capture that elusive "buzz" factor. I love creativity, and I'm wide open to whatever idea you want to float. But at the same time, it's important to understand the difference between a gimmick and an original, enduring idea.

Gimmicks are about short-term gain, not long-term relationships. They get attention, but do they really change people's thinking? Some pastors seem almost addicted to the attention gimmicks bring. As a result, they look for the most outrageous sermon themes or advertising ideas. But in a culture where sexually charged and provocative advertising escalates almost daily, trying to shock an audience with a racy church billboard doesn't really pack much of a punch anymore.

Gimmicks can be dangerous. And I'm not talking about falling off that two-story perch. I'm talking about the fact that what's funny to you might be offensive or hurtful to others. In 2010, Spirit Airlines launched the "Check the Oil on Our Beaches" ad campaign, trying to humorously promote beach destinations untouched by the BP oil spill. But the company was remarkably tone deaf to the hundreds of thousands whose jobs were lost and lives devastated by the tragic spill. The public was not amused, and the campaign was quickly pulled.

Gimmicks often backfire. Instead of generating positive press, they often create criticism. Trying to be edgy and cool, McDonalds released its "I'd Hit It" campaign, thinking the phrase meant "choosing it." But the street phrase actually means something much more provocative. Millions of moms did not approve.

Gimmicks can cheapen your perception and reputation. Ultimately, do you want to be known as a pastor, teacher, or leader who taught the Word and timeless principles that impacted lives, or as "the guy who preached a sermon in his boxer shorts"?

I've spent my career helping churches, ministries, and nonprofits become more creative in the way they engage today's cluttered and distracted culture. I'm certainly not against innovative methods to share your story. Explore unusual ideas. Break some artistic boundaries.

But don't do it at the expense of a gimmick that could undermine you and your church's credibility and impact.

GUESS WHAT? BILLBOARDS STILL WORK

Years ago, billboards were all the rage for businesses around the world. While billboards date back to ancient Egypt, they really came alive in America back in the 1950s when vacations by car became so popular. Churches eventually jumped on the bandwagon, but in the digital age, most churches have shifted advertising to online platforms.

But according to numerous sources, businesses are betting big on billboards once again. In fact, in 2019, it was the only major non-digital category in advertising that was growing. The irony about all this is major technology companies like Netflix, Alibaba, and Google are now all investing in billboards.

What do they know that churches should know? It appears that in today's cluttered digital era driving a car is one of the only times during the day when we aren't staring at screens—which means we're starting to notice billboards again. Sure we can listen to music or podcasts in the car, but when it comes to our visual attention, billboards are making an impact.

And from a cost perspective, the advertising impact is pretty high for billboards. Plus today, we have the advent of "smart" billboards that can aggregate data from multiple sources, and use digital screens to update information.

The bottom line is that it may be time to rethink using billboards to help remind people that your church is pretty awesome!

WHAT YOU SHOULD EXPECT FROM A CHURCH WEBSITE

The world of website development has come so far that there's very little you can't do online these days. But in spite of the progress—including easy-to-build websites based on templates (many of which are free or inexpensive)—churches, ministries, and nonprofit organizations still struggle getting their websites to accomplish their goals.

Sometimes it's an expectation problem (because after all, like most other subjects in this book they don't teach website development in seminary or Bible college) and sometimes it's a lack of good advice. Either way, I've created a baseline list of what your website should be able to do. And if it doesn't, you need to have a serious talk with your in-house webmaster or your outside vendor:

Your website should work. Sure there are times when sites or servers have issues, but they should be few and far between. If your site malfunctions on a regular basis, something is wrong. Don't allow your webmaster or outside vendor to make excuses. If they can't get it running smoothly on a regular basis, it's time to look for another vendor.

You should be able to manage it in-house. With the exception of major design or technical changes, there's no reason you should have to "submit a request" for changes on your site and then wait for the vendor to follow up. Most day-to-day "admin" activities like posting blogs or videos, updating photos, new pages, changing store products, and more should all be done by your internal team. If your vendor is forcing you to submit requests for everything, then they're just looking for ways to make more money—period.

Your online store or donation engine should work. In the early days, e-commerce was hit or miss, but today, there are plenty of options that work very well. If your church or ministry is relying on product sales or encouraging donations, then it should be easy, streamlined, and simple to do. If people are trying to buy or donate and can't do it, then it's time to look for another service.

You should be notified whenever anything goes wrong. If a donation can't be processed for any reason, a software update is required, or any other issue, you should get an immediate notification. I spoke to a church recently who said the only way they know their donor page isn't working is when a potential donor calls to let them know. That's embarrassing and antiquated. Make sure you're getting notified of any problem so you can fix it now.

Your website should work beautifully on mobile devices. Mobile isn't the future, it's already here, so your videos, online store, donation engine, blog, and more should all work just fine from mobile devices. And I'm not simply talking about what's called "responsive"—which is simply shrinking everything down—I'm talking about truly thinking through how the content is presented in mobile environments.

Finally, be skeptical of "maintenance fees." I know some churches that have paid monthly fees to web companies for years and received little or nothing in return. When software needs updating or occasional problems happen, fine. There are also monthly fees for issues like server hosting, but much beyond that, you should never be held hostage to outside companies charging you monthly fees.

What do you do if you're experiencing any of these issues?

It's time for a "come to Jesus" meeting with your webmaster or Internet vendor. In today's online world, power surges, server problems, and other things happen, but not often. You need a reliable website, so be very leery of excuses.

Make sure your website provider has a great track record. Talk to their other customers—particularly other churches, ministries, or nonprofits. Ask tough questions. Find out how well their websites function. References matter.

Make sure your website can deliver what you need. Live streaming, video on demand, blogs, social media options—whatever your ministry needs, your website should be able to deliver.

Don't wait. I know churches that put up with problems for months or years. But the truth is, every day your website isn't functioning properly, you're losing potential visitors, donors, or product sales. My experience indicates that virtually 100 percent of potential new visitors to your church will check you out online first. When it's that important, you can't afford to not have your website perform.

Last, and perhaps most important—hire a team that's a partner *instead* of just a *vendor*. A partner has the ministry's best interests in mind (not finding ways to bill more money for features the church doesn't need) and will work with you to find the best way to accomplish the church's vision.

> **At the end of the day, the website is another tool for communicating vision (just like the weekend service), so it's important the experience online reflects the same level of excellence the church strives for everywhere else.**

In the 21st century, church and ministry websites should work. It's time to stop with the excuses, so find a vendor or webmaster you have confidence in, then build an easy to use site with a compelling design, and watch your ministry grow.

WHY YOUR WEBSITE NEEDS A STRATEGY

During the development of your church or ministry website, you should be thinking about how good your web strategy really is and how it impacts your audience, supporters, or partners. From a strategy point of view, here are some things to consider about your organization's web presence:

The design may be terrific, but from a strategy perspective, make sure it's not confusing because it's overly busy, or all the flashy stuff is distracting. Consider the layout based on the audience. For instance, a blog seeks to gain an ongoing conversation with your readers—meaning it's alive with new updates, and gives the audience a platform for an ongoing discussion.

From a donation perspective, the "donation" or "give" button should be clear and easy to find—otherwise most surfers could actually miss it. Website visitors are "impulse" people, and if they can't easily find what they're looking for, they'll give up and move on to something else.

If you list numerous "events" on the home page, consider consolidating under an "Events" icon that takes the viewer to all those different events, leaving the home page cleaner and simpler.

Talk to your web team and ask the question—what is the *main* purpose of this site? What could this site accomplish for us? Then build it according to those goals.

Keep in mind, we're talking *strategy* which will affect *design*. The question now is how do we make the site come alive, while keeping it simple and easy to navigate, so the user can find what he's looking for quickly, and donate and/or purchase products easily. We've learned that most web surfers are driven by impulse, and if the site is too busy or is distracting, they'll easily forget why they came. That's why I'd like to make it really easy for the surfer to do what he came to the site to accomplish.

Also, be careful about "bouncing" people to other sites for video and other experiences. I'm not interested in driving people to someone else's website. For instance, if you do streaming video, let's make it originate in your domain and keep your users within your boundaries.

The key that drives me is *connection*. We want to be able to connect with our congregation, visitors, partners, or audience in every possible platform in order to position you as an organization of the future.

WEBSITE DESIGN: FLYING BOXES DON'T IMPRESS ME

We live in the age of Marvel movies, special effects that blow the mind, and virtual reality. Am I really supposed to be impressed with the flying boxes, twirling logos, other effects on your website? People who come to your website are looking for *information*, not *entertainment*. They want to know who you are, what you're about, and how you can impact their lives.

The statistics of how quickly web surfers expect you to provide those answers would freak you out. That's why when that hourglass, clock, or status bar shows up indicating we're waiting for something fancy to happen, we move elsewhere.

Design is important, but if the design makes it more difficult to get the information I need, then forget it. I can get my thrills at other places. On your website, give me what I need to know.

HOW TO WRITE A BIOGRAPHY FOR YOUR WEBSITE

During your career, you'll have plenty of opportunities to write a biography about yourself for websites, social media, conference programs, membership in professional organizations, and more. The problem is, too many people seize that moment to pontificate about themselves as if they'd won an Academy Award or Nobel Prize. But writing an effective bio can do more than just tout your accomplishments—it can really serve to advance your ideas and message. Now's a good time to rethink your bio, and here's a handful of important principles to keep in mind:

1. **Mention your accomplishments but don't go over the top.** Far too many bios include phrases like "changing the world," "best-selling author," "in demand speaker," or "internationally respected _____." Unless those types of accolades can be verified, don't stretch the truth. It hurts your credibility. Never forget that in the Internet age, everything can be verified.

2. **Focus on "One Big Thing."** Too many bios list a wide array of interests and work, and leave the reader wondering what your area of expertise actually is. Instead, use your bio to share what you feel called and prepared to accomplish with your life. (And if you don't know what that is, then read my book: *One Big Thing: Discovering What You Were Born to Do.*)

3. **Write your bio for a specific audience.** Is the bio being used for your website? Then focus on potential visitors checking out your church. A leadership conference? Then focus on your expertise in that area. For a job site? Focus on your qualifications. For a professional organization? Make it clear why you're part of that group. Always think about the specific reader of the bio and what they need to know.

4. **Keep it short and sweet.** The most qualified speakers don't need to promote themselves in their bio. Keep it short and focused on the purpose at hand.

5. **If you're young or haven't accomplished a great deal, then don't fake it.** When someone starts a new career, they often feel like there isn't much to say. If that's the case, then make what little you've done look good. And think about things outside the workplace to talk about—maybe your work for a local cause or nonprofit. Don't be afraid to sell yourself, but don't make things up. Your integrity matters, so just keep it simple.

6. **Finally, have some fun.** When reporter Paula Zahn joked on CNN that I was "the only working producer in Hollywood with a Ph.D. in Theology," I included that in my bio. The only reason my wife agreed to go out with me on our first date is that when I called her, she thought I was someone else—so I've used that in a bio. Maybe you have an odd hobby, or a quirky past. Don't be serious all the time. People will enjoy seeing your personality.

Your biography isn't about bragging rights, it's about credibility. Why should I listen to your message, check out your website, or connect with you online? Lose the hype, be authentic, and have some fun.

KEY PRINCIPLES TO CONSIDER ABOUT MARKETING, COMMUNICATION, AND YOUR WEBSITE:

1. **Marketing and communication are team sports. As you grow your church or ministry, invest in a great team.** In a world where capturing people's attention is so important, a great creative team will help you grow. You can't do everything yourself so surround yourself with a team who can help.

2. **Your church website should be primarily focused on potential visitors.** Your website isn't for church members—they already show up and know about the Christmas event, the youth concert, or when services start. Make it easy on your site for a new visitor to find out who you are, where you are, what time your services begin, and why they should visit.

3. **Understand that your Sunday message is the priority message for everything you communicate all week.** Redundancy builds trust and drives the message in deep. When you aim all your communication guns in one direction it makes a huge impact, so get everyone on the same team, and get them following the lead of the pastor.

4. **Experiment and try new things.** Effective communication is about experimenting and trying new ideas and approaches. You never know what will create a breakthrough until you give it a shot so start encouraging your team to worry less about failure and more about creative thinking.

5. **Take your website seriously, because it's far more important than you realize.** It's your "communication hub" which should be the

primary place people will go to find information about your church or ministry.

6. **Your website should work—virtually all the time.** Websites are relatively simple and easy to design these days so don't allow your webmaster or outside vendor to make excuses. If they can't get it running smoothly on a regular basis, it's time to look for another vendor.

7. **It should be easy for people to donate money through your website and mobile platform.** More and more people today are using online payment systems, so you need to have that option. If people are trying to buy products or donate and can't do it online, then they'll often give to another church or ministry. It's worth remembering that when the church lockdown happened in 2020 because of the Coronavirus, the churches with the highest rates of online giving before the crisis were the churches that survived the best financially.

8. **Your website should work beautifully on mobile devices.** Mobile is now, and your videos, online store, donation engine, blog, and more should all work just fine from mobile devices.

— 7 —

SOCIAL MEDIA

"Content is fire. Social media is gasoline."

—Jay Baer

While there is more to life than simply growing your social media following, the impact you can have on followers is enormous. Whether you have five or five hundred thousand social media followers, there's an important secret I've learned. In my experience, one of the biggest reasons people follow you on social media is:

People want to know what it's like to be you.

Simple as that. Particularly if you're a leader, most people can't just call you up and meet over coffee. But when you reveal the "inside" story of your life via social media, it's a similar experience. Honestly, it's time to encourage, enlighten, and inspire your followers instead of taking photos of your lunch or letting them know you're at Starbucks.

In other words, tell me the real story about your challenges, obstacles, frustrations, and victories. Give me an insider's look at your job. For instance, if you're a pastor, tell me about your struggles developing a new sermon series. If you're a speaker, tell me about your jitters backstage before you speak. If you're a teacher, tell me about your hardest challenges and how you overcame them.

We hear surface stories all day long. What we're looking for is *insight*. It's not about bragging, but about sharing things that only you know. Strategies, tactics, and techniques you've experienced the hard way. The secrets of your successes—and your failures.

Most people aren't interested in shallow opinions, unformed thoughts, or glib motivational quotes. What they're looking for is the inside story.

And that's the story only you can tell . . .

HOW TO FIND YOUR SOCIAL MEDIA VOICE

Finding your authentic voice in social media isn't that different from traditional media. I had a client once who was a TV host. The problem was, as soon as the red light came on the camera, he became a completely different person. His voice got deeper. His style became bigger. He was more over the top. It just wasn't him. Even his friends would tell him, "Stop using your TV voice." But many of us do the same thing on social media. We try to project authority, sound more spiritual, or generally be someone we're not. Remember my age-old branding advice—a brand isn't about becoming something (or someone) else, it's about discovering who you really are. With that in mind—here's my advice about finding the real you on social media:

1. Don't say things on social media you wouldn't say to someone face to face. I have a friend that suddenly becomes totally "spiritual" on social media. He blurts out cheesy cornball Christian sayings he'd never actually say to anyone face to face. Others become hyper political, or try to be overly inspiring. If that's not you when you're *off* social media, then my advice is to drop it when you're *on* social media.

2. Think about your own personality. Do you love jokes? Make people happy? Think about more serious things? Love sports? Keep that personality online. People like you because you're unique, so stop trying to be someone else. Make sure that if your followers didn't know it was you, they'd be able to figure it out just by your subject matter, writing style, and online personality.

3. Write about the One Big Thing in your life. Just like I write about in my book, *One Big Thing: Discovering What You Were Born to Do*, discovering the One Thing that defines you, that you're passionate about, and that you love, is the key to discovering your purpose—and developing your brand. If you haven't read the book, I'd encourage you to get it right away. Once you find that unique niche, then your voice becomes defined, and you'll start getting noticed.

You can stay frustrated that few people are following you on social media, or start rethinking your unique voice. It's not something you make up—it's something you are. Find it and start getting heard.

HOW TO SHARE YOUR FAITH ON SOCIAL MEDIA

I find it fascinating that many people who handle social media for very large churches and ministries find it difficult to share their faith on their personal social media platforms. And many who do, manage to do it in a pretty obnoxious way. But every new technology gives us another possibility for telling the greatest story ever told, but we have to do it with honesty and sincerity.

Krysta Masciale, Executive Brand Strategist, puts it this way: "For me, it's important that I share as much on social media as I would in person. Since I don't speak about my faith until I've gained trust and been given permission to do so in a relationship, I use that same philosophy with my social media accounts. Also, know your audience. If Christians follow you and are expecting spiritual insights, *give it to them*. If not, be aware that you're building a relationship, not trying to sell a car."

Krysta is exactly right. So I asked Kristen Tarsiuk, Creative Director at CRISTA Ministries in Seattle, to give us some suggestions about sharing our faith online in a way that makes an impact. Kristen and her husband Justin are also church planters so she brings very relevant insight to the issue:

Social media can be an extremely powerful tool, or it can be noise. It can be a celebration of the goodness of God, or a polished promotion of self. The choice is always ours. Here are three tips on how to share your faith on social media authentically.

Be relatable. As a creative director and pastor, I could post pics of fun production meetings or moments of me in a picturesque café studying God's Word as I prepare to deliver Sunday's message. My life as church-planting, creative director is unique, but it is significantly less relatable to most people. So, for the past few years, I have chosen to share my journey of faith as a mom on social media. It never fails, each week the stories I post of my son are conversation starters with other moms around the world, but more importantly my son's school. What I post opens the door for trust and connection, and ultimately me sharing my reliance on Jesus. Ask yourself, "Is what I am sharing relatable to nonbelievers?" Not every post needs to point to the gospel, but think about the story you are telling.

Be human. Don't be afraid to share those less than perfect moments of life, especially the ones when you personally need God to show up. Christians suffer. Nonbelievers suffer. Pain and suffering are a universal experience.

A few years ago, my three-year-old son had bladder surgery for a condition he had since birth. My husband and I utilized our social feeds to share our journey. In post-op recovery we did a "Praise God—this journey is over!" type of post, thanking God for His goodness and faithfulness.

A few hours after arriving home (off the high of the Praise God post), Rocco's temperature skyrocketed. We quickly found ourselves speeding through the streets of Manhattan to get Rocco to the emergency room. At 2 a.m. we shared our pain and asked for prayers. At 3 a.m., the fever broke. Then what we thought would be a short recovery, turned into weeks, with multiple posts saying things still aren't working.

I remember thinking, I don't want to be Debbie the Downer. Do people really want to know my son's bladder is still not working? When we shared updates on social media, both our Christian and non-Christian friends would reach out letting us know we were in their thoughts and prayers. And when we shared the good news that Rocco was healed (almost four weeks later)—both our Christians and non-Christian friends celebrated with us.

During the COVID-19 quarantine, two videographer friends of mine created a daily video of their experience in New York City on Facebook and Instagram. They shared their conversations with family, struggle to talk to a human at the unemployment office, online game nights, the boredom, the fear, and the gratitude for small things like a bag of chips.

I reached out to them to say thank you, and that I looked forward to their daily post. I also opened up about a significant loss our family had just experienced. My friend responded and said, "I really appreciate you reaching out to us. It makes me feel less alone knowing that we're all going through pain in a different way."

Be humble and human. Share the less than perfect moments of life. Share your suffering in a healthy way. Our weaknesses are the perfect platforms for God's strength. Share that story.

Be mindful. Remember, someone is always listening, and on social—always watching, liking, and sharing. The Apostle Paul wrote, "'I have the right to do anything,' you say—but not everything is beneficial. 'I have the right to do anything'—but not everything is constructive. No one should seek their own good, but the good of others" (1 Corinthians 10:23-24).

Yes, we have the right to emotionally process and share our opinions on social media. But is it beneficial? Yes, we can post selfies and polished pics of ourselves. But is it constructive?

I have watched leaders bring pain to people by posting their opinion on social media—not understanding the weight of the conversation they entered, or the hashtag they used. Social media is only as powerful as the change it creates. If you use your social media to raise awareness, (which is a good thing to do!) make sure to back it up with action, and educate yourself before entering the conversation.

I am saddened when I see leaders post the less relatable moments of ministry life (often from a stage or green room) that can easily be taken out of context. Please, remember *everything communicates*. And thanks to social media, almost anything you say, anything you wear, and anywhere you go can end up on social media too.

We now have social accounts dedicated to documenting the unique and expensive lifestyles of today's pastors and leaders. Regardless of where the blessing came from, how hard you work, the sacrifices your family has made (trust me, I get it as a pastor and a wife of a pastor's kid)—we have to ask ourselves, are we sharing our life in a way that truly seeks the good of others? Is our story pointing people to the Gospel, or distracting people from it?

We are called to be a light. We have to be mindful of how we present ourselves as leaders. It is so important that we think before we post. Let's not lose our testimony over a post, hashtag, or flippant tweet, and let's not let our lifestyle distract from the gospel.

Be relatable, be human, and be mindful. Leverage social media as a tool of influence and a tool for sharing your faith.

SOCIAL MEDIA IS SOCIAL

It may seem obvious, but I've found that too many leaders and their organizations think that by posting on a regular basis, they're engaging in social media. But afterwards, if you're not responding back to what your followers are saying, you couldn't be more mistaken. Let me give you a great example of how one company gets it right:

A year or so ago, I flew to Orlando on American Airlines. Once I sat down and pulled out a novel, I realized my reading lamp wasn't working. Obviously it's tough to check hundreds of thousands of reading lights across the fleet, so I brought it to their attention.

I tweeted: "@AmericanAir—check todays Flight 0244 seat 10C. The overhead light doesn't work. Thanks!"

Literally, within minutes (and before we even took off) American responded with a Twitter post: "@philcooke—Our apologies, Phil. We'll report the light issue so that it can be repaired."

That kind of immediate response tells their customers that American cares enough about customers to monitor their social media traffic and respond, plus—they listened and will fix the problem. That kind of engagement can build a lot of credibility—especially during a crisis.

It's worth mentioning that when a serious problem happens and people post upsetting or negative remarks on social media, you can often give them a phone number or e-mail address and take the criticism offline to deal with privately.

What about YOUR church or ministry? Are you listening to your congregation, visitors, or donors, or are you just using social media as a soapbox to preach or sell?

I recently showed a local pastor how important responding to his followers could be. Once he started doing it, one church member posted on Facebook that her pastor responded to her question and how great she thought it was and how much she loved the church.

Social media isn't a one-way street. American Airlines, and now my pastor friend, both get that.

YOUR SOCIAL MEDIA PROFILE IS MORE IMPORTANT THAN YOU THINK

When it comes to a "profile" or "bio" on social media, most people just have fun with it. That's OK, but if you want to be an influencer, get noticed, or grow your followers, a more creative and strategic profile can give you a big boost. Here are the three most important areas most people need to fix:

1. **Your Photo:** What's the image you want to project to the world? It's not about egomania, it's about perception. Your social media profile photo is something people will see over and over again—perhaps thousands of times. So make it something you want burned into their memory. Great visual design is the gateway that opens your world to outsiders. Photos are an important part of great visual design, therefore every time you post a photo on a profile, make it count.

2. **The Link:** What's the most important and authoritative website that tells your story? Do you have a blog? A church or personal website? In some cases, you may want to use the link to your church, ministry, or nonprofit—particularly if you focus your social media posts on the work you do with that organization. Whatever URL it may be, it's the key to your followers finding out more about you, so don't forget it.

3. **Your Bio:** As I've said in an earlier chapter, keep it short, but make it count. If you had one sentence to share who you are and what you do with the public, what would you say? You can have fun with it, but at the same time it's one of the most visible opportunities for you to connect with people.

Keep in mind that these tips work for organizations as well. The bottom line is that an informative social media profile makes a big impact on your perception and the perception of your church, ministry, or nonprofit.

DOES YOUR SOCIAL MEDIA INFORMATION MATCH YOUR MESSAGE?

I met someone recently who wanted to be taken seriously as a Christian apologist. He hoped to increase his opportunities to speak and teach to larger audiences, and land a publishing deal in the process. But when I checked his social media platforms, here's what I found:

-> *His Facebook banner photo was a shot of him fishing. (Apparently he likes to fish.)*

-> *His Twitter background photo was his favorite football team.*

-> *His Twitter bio was a Vince Lombardi quote: "We would accomplish many more things if we did not think of them as impossible."*

All very nice. Except none of it had anything to do with his personal brand. If you want to be taken seriously as an apologist, pastor, nonprofit leader, writer, worship leader—whatever—you need to be easily discoverable. That means all your social media, website, blog and other information needs to support the perception you're trying to convey to your audience.

Confusion carries a hefty price tag because increasingly, job offers, opportunities to speak, news coverage, donors, publishers and more search for your information online and via social media. And if it's not clear, they'll look for someone else.

> Don't waste your digital real estate by squandering promotional opportunities via social media.

Aim all your promotional guns in a single direction, by making sure your online, blog, and social media information point to your expertise and personal brand. Sure a Twitter photo of a kitten is cute, but if you're serious about your career and calling, I would suggest the right photo of you would accomplish much more.

WHAT EXACTLY IS A "STRATEGY"?

Thousands of churches, ministries, and nonprofits are using social media today, but in far too many cases, these unique tools are being used at random, which completely wastes their power. For most organizations, sometimes it works, other times it doesn't—which leads to the big question—what is "strategy" to begin with?

The word "strategy" came into the English language around 1810, and by contrast, "tactics" came into use two hundred years earlier. People had discussed "tactics," but it wasn't until 1810 that Carl Von Clausewitz began using it in battle. He outlined three basic steps:

1. Figure out where you are (Point A).
2. Decide where you want to be (Point B).
3. Create a plan to get from A to B.

It's incredibly simple, but it's surprising how few people—particularly in media—actually take the time to consider those steps and come up with the best solution. In case after case, when I ask church or ministry social media teams about *strategy*, they reply with *tactics*. But tactics are the tools that get you there, not the goal you're trying to achieve.

It's important to know the difference.

If you're involved in communicating a message at any level and are expecting results, then you need to understand how it works. It simply means having a plan about what exactly you want to accomplish, how you intend to make it happen, and how you measure the results.

It's not about random tweeting, nice Instagram photos, or posting Facebook messages. We should always start with a goal. Is it evangelism? Church growth? Building a sense of community? Raising money? Establishing your expertise? Promoting your organization's work? Whatever the strategy is, "tactics" become the practical steps it will take to reach that goal.

In my personal case, my blog, my podcast, my YouTube channel, my speaking topics, and my social media platforms all revolve around the intersection of faith, media, and culture. I rarely post about politics, sports, recipes, or anything else—unless it relates to media, faith, and culture. After all, there are far more expert people than me to comment on other things, but I've spent my adult life exploring the intersection of faith, media, and culture. That's why people follow my social media platforms, listen to my podcast, come hear me speak, and read my blog or books.

The question is—what's the subject, experience, or area about which people want to hear from you? What's the issue that you bring a unique perspective to? The old saying is right, "If you don't know where you're going, you'll never know when you arrive."

Social media isn't just about *promotion*, it's also about *ministry*.

Establishing your presence and voice on social media, or sharing sermon quotes are all important, but it's only half the equation. Just as important is using social media to actually minister to people. For instance, you can search within a twenty-mile radius of your church for hashtags like #movingday, #newintown, or #depressed. Then reach out to those people with a welcome, an invitation to church, an offer to pray, talk on the phone, or meet in person.

Social media isn't *passive*, it's *active*, and I can't overemphasize that it's a two-way conversation. No matter how great your ideas, if you're only sending content out, then you're missing the point. Have your team scan social media posts in your area looking for people struggling, lonely, divorced, or searching for answers.

How your church responds could be the most powerful social media strategy of all.

DOES SOCIAL MEDIA INFLUENCE TRANSLATE INTO $$?

The short answer is not for most people. In a recent conversation with a major movie marketer, he told me that although one of his recent studio projects had three million Facebook fans, the movie did dismal box office business. On the other hand, we're seeing more and more bloggers and social media mavens snagging big bucks in exchange for promoting products and projects. I noticed someone from Toronto recently earned a free flight to New Zealand based on her manic blogging. Other social media users are being rewarded with weekends in Vegas and other resort cities for pushing products or causes.

Various social media apps try to rate social media "influence" based on numbers and connections of followers. And companies are scanning these results to find people who can help them share their story. Our team has been doing some fascinating projects creating live online webcasts for clients and mobilizing social media followers to important causes.

But does it directly translate to financial success? There's not a lot of support for that hope, although these and other examples show me two things:

1. **Significant numbers of people can become engaged in online conversations about products, people, and issues, which can spawn new ideas, trends, and even movements.**

2. **Anyone can now become an influencer.** Engage online enough—with interesting and focused content—and you'll start to create a following.

My perspective is that social media still falls under marketing and advertising. It's not really much different than a billboard, TV commercial, or print ad, with the exception of one big thing:

It talks back. *It's social.*

Which means that we now have an advertising platform that closes the loop. It's not just about sharing your message as a one-way proposition. Today through social media, we can get a response almost immediately. It may not translate to dollars at that moment—but then again, what other advertising medium does that?

Plus, what a powerful way to build a tribe and get your story or message out there? What you do with that following is up to you.

STOP OBSESSING OVER SOCIAL MEDIA METRICS AND START OBSESSING OVER IDEAS

Which leads to my opinion that a great mistake of the social media age is obsessing over metrics at the expense of ideas. There are so many digital tools today that analyze our posts on Facebook, Twitter, Instagram, and other platforms that we've become mesmerized at numbers rather than impact.

But wait—before you say numbers *are* impact—let me explain:

I'm noticing the situation with many church, ministry and nonprofit communication teams who constantly remind the pastor or leader about the organization's social media metrics. With great enthusiasm, they do their best to impress leadership with followers, engagements, and other positive stats.

That's nice, and don't get me wrong—we do want people interacting and engaging with your posts, and we want to understand more about how that engagement happens.

However, I'd also like to see more communication teams sweating the message.

Yes—it's the pastor or leader's job to come up with the message, and the communication team's job to share and measure it. However, don't get so caught up with tracking that you start ignoring other important issues of creativity and relevance.

As we've seen many times, when it comes to metrics, gaming the system is pretty easy. There are plenty ways to jack up the numbers, sell more of the pastor's books, buy followers, or otherwise make the social media numbers look great.

But my question is simple:

What are we saying? What is the message we're sharing? What's the relevance of that message? What's the level of the writing, the creativity, or the thinking behind it?

Has the fact that someone clicked on your scripture post actually changed their life? I would far rather have a small group of enthusiastic social media followers than a massive group of followers who don't really care. Find your voice. Deliver compelling messages. Create posts that people can't forget.

Focus less on hitting metrics, and more on changing people's lives.

HOW TO RESPOND TO CRITICS ON SOCIAL MEDIA

If you're accomplishing anything of significance in the world, you're bound to pick up a few critics. Especially in today's social media maelstrom, there are plenty of people who are more than happy to criticize just about anything—especially from the comfort of hiding behind a fake social media name. Sometimes the critics are clearly off their rocker, but in many cases, the critic has a legitimate complaint, and occasionally it hurts. The question is, how do we respond? Do we ignore it or do we respond? Here are a few principles that might help the next time you get a critic (serious or otherwise) on social media:

First of all, take a breath. Don't respond immediately out of your emotions. You'll almost always regret it, and often you'll say something in the heat of the moment that you'll regret later. How many politicians, famous athletes, CEO's, or ministry leaders have been forced to step down because of a thoughtless response to a critic on social media? Far too many. Just take a breath, step back, and think.

Check his or her number of followers. I recently received a scathing social media response to a blog post of mine. Before I responded, I checked how many people were following him. It was four. That's right—four people. For me to respond to him meant I would reveal his name to my thousands of social media followers. In other words, I'd just be promoting him. That's why I decided to ignore it since only four people (besides me) saw it anyway. (And sometimes when you ignore critics, it drives them crazy.)

Don't always assume they're out to get you. Think about the criticism from their perspective. Perhaps he or she misread your post, or didn't think it through. I've had many critics who changed their mind when I (graciously) pointed out their incorrect interpretation.

If it's legitimate, take it. In my own case, I freely admit that I've posted things I wish I hadn't, or wish my writing had been more clear. In those cases, I willingly took the bullet. A critic can do you a lot of good if it's solid criticism, if you take it to heart, and if you reflect on how you could have done better.

Finally, if it's a jerk, ignore it. Some people are desperate for attention, and while they're sitting in their parent's basement in their pajamas, they decide to attack someone online. It makes them feel powerful, but in reality, it's a cowardly, miserable act, so don't go down to their level. Just walk away.

I can't tell you the number of highly respected leaders who gambled with their reputation and integrity because they got caught up in a pointless, emotional argument online. Don't take the bait. People are watching you respond (or not respond) which is why you should make sure everything you post is something you'd be proud of later.

HOW TO DEAL WITH ONLINE CHURCH TROLLS

Now that we've discussed critics, let's take a deep dive into an entirely new world: online trolls. I've consulted with hundreds of churches over the years, and sadly, there's one common enemy some of the most effective churches in America share—*online trolls*. In these cases, at least one disgruntled ex-church member or ex-employee has decided to launch a Facebook page, Twitter feed, and in some cases a blog with the express purpose of criticizing the church. There are many reasons: some were offended by the pastor, others don't like the church's teaching, a few feel they were taken advantage of, and still others are convinced they've uncovered secret wrongdoing within church leadership.

It's actually shocking to see the number of Christians who feel "called" to be a theology cop and are willing to brutally criticize other believers (or entire churches) they've never met or attended in the name of "sound theology."

I'm all for helping correct poor biblical interpretation,
but it appears in far too many cases,
most of these critics enjoy it a bit too much.

There's no question that some pastors and churches do dumb things, a handful do the wrong things, and a few do illegal things. But the question is—whether it's true or not, is a social media platform or a blog the place to air the dirty laundry?

B.F.—Before Facebook, gossip was a similar option, but thankfully, most just left the particular church. In my case, over the years there have been plenty of churches and pastors I disagreed with, but I didn't gossip or launch a Twitter campaign to complain, I made a decision to either pursue the issue with church leadership or just move on.

But maybe "moving on" is the problem for these critics. They just can't let go of the hurt or being offended. From being on the inside of many of these situations and having read the critical posts, I can say the vast majority aren't acting out of a biblical perspective, they're simply acting out. Because they feel they were wronged, they're lashing out at the church or the pastor.

That's why in the same way I advise against organized online campaigns against Hollywood, the gay community, or anyone else; and I would say the same thing to people who launch online campaigns against churches: They make little to no impact, and do nothing for the cause of Christ.

Besides—think for a minute:

Someone who feels wronged by a local church or pastor, and invests the incredible amount of time it takes to create a blog and fill it with criticism, or do the same with a social media platform—and keep it going for months or years—probably has much bigger problems in their life.

Now keep in mind that I'm not talking about the occasional critic here, I'm talking about an attack by an unrepentant troll. If you're a pastor or leader in a church who's undergoing this kind of persistent online criticism, here are my suggestions:

Before you react, consider the source. There's a difference between the occasional online critic and a troll. Most pastors know these people because in many cases, they're ex-church members or employees. On the other hand, you may see a post—or even criticism—from a church member who has an innocent question that you can easily answer, and which solves the problem. So know the difference.

If it's a troll, ignore it. I tracked one online troll who had positioned himself as a theology cop and had been ripping into a local pastor for months. He only had five Twitter followers (probably his family), which means he had little to no impact. As I said earlier in the case of my critic, that's not worth a response.

Don't help him by responding. When you respond on a social media platform, you're sharing the troll with all your followers which is a victory for *him*. Plus, for most trolls, that validates their efforts. Don't help promote him or her by responding.

Finally, stop reading it. I know some pastors who dwell so much on their online criticism it derails their concentration. Eventually they become depressed and lost focus on their ministry. Stop obsessing over the 3 percent who are critics and start feeding the 97 percent who aren't. Particularly with social media platforms, trolls are easy to block.

Today we live in a culture of victimization. For some people, they've essentially discovered their identity in being a victim, so they're willing to invest a great deal in expressing that victimhood. Stop reading the criticism, and start leading the congregation or ministry team. The dog may bark, but the train keeps on rolling. Church doctrine, theology, and moral living are critically important, but never forget there are legitimate ways of correction within a church.

Becoming an online troll isn't one.

SHOULD YOU CONSIDER A LAWSUIT OVER A NEGATIVE SOCIAL MEDIA POST?

Let's go a step further. Is there a point where you should consider a lawsuit or take other legal action? Outside the United States, it's almost open season on employees who post negative content about their job on social media—largely because freedom of speech isn't such a valued principle as it is in the United States. In fact, defamation is becoming a huge issue on social media sites and legal action is dramatically increasing internationally. In Canada, 15 percent of all Web 2.0 rulings were on defamation cases. In France, it's 49 percent.

However, here in the U.S. employers are experiencing real challenges when they try to sue employees—even when those employees are critical of the companies they work for. Even when people use social media to post negative news about the organization, or get drunk and post something highly disparaging, it's a real challenge to pursue them in court.

> Even in the rare cases where an organization
> wins a social media lawsuit, they can
> still lose the PR battle. In other words,
> in the social media world, tread very carefully.

It's the Wild West out there, with lots of potential minefields for organizations of all types. For instance, someone could potentially sue a boss for sexual harassment after he repeatedly tries to "friend" him or her on Facebook. Or employers might pull a job offer after learning personal information from an applicant's social media site.

All kinds of things—religious affiliation, activism, political positions, and more are suddenly in the public domain and bound to be seen by potential and current employers. But lawsuits against employees and others have proven to be very difficult to win. In a 2009 case, one company sued employees over comments on a social media page that they felt violated their core values. But not only did they lose, they were required to pay the employees thousands of dollars in damages.

Here's my advice:

First—get the right counsel from an attorney who understands social media, and advice from social media or public relations experts. It's tricky stuff, and the old rules about office behavior and how to respond don't necessarily apply.

Second—jump into the stream of social media yourself. Learn the unwritten rules about online behavior—what's considered personal, public, serious, and funny. Otherwise, you'll blunder into a huge (and expensive) legal misstep. It doesn't matter if you consider yourself a "traditional" media expert. Social media has turned everything on its head.

Finally—Understand that PR has changed in a digital age. Traditional press releases don't make nearly the splash as strategic blog posts or social media posts. In a social media world, the nexus of influence is changing, and you need to stay on top of that change.

CAN A CHURCH OR MINISTRY DO ANYTHING ABOUT AN EMPLOYEE'S NEGATIVE SOCIAL MEDIA POSTS?

You may have seen that recently, police departments and law-enforcement unions are issuing warnings and offering social media training to members, hoping to stop a recent tide of offensive posts. There's apparently been a wide range of controversial posts, from disgruntled employees complaining about policies, to threats, and even racist comments.

There have been numerous cases where church or ministry employees complained online about their pastor's message, a particular policy, or coworkers. Whatever the reason, it's not a positive thing—particularly when they're seen by the general public. It tends to toss the biblical concept of "unity" out the window when local communities see church employees complain, disrespect, or criticize the church or its leaders.

A number of major churches and ministry organizations have a social media policy in place, but not many. Besides, are they legal? Can a church censor those posts, or fire the employee? What about freedom of speech?

I asked my friend David Middlebrook, a highly respected attorney who focuses on church and nonprofit issues. Here's David's response:

> Courts have ruled that the information posted on Facebook or other social media websites is not entitled to special privacy protections in legal proceedings despite the use of software privacy settings. For example, in 2012, the United States District Court of California noted information posted on social media platforms is not protected by common law privacy protections. Mailhoit v. Home Depot U.S.A. Inc., 285 F.R.D. 566, 570 (C.D. Cal. 2012). Other court decisions across the country echo this ruling.

> Every church should have a staff handbook ("Handbook") signed by all of its employees, volunteers, and board members ("Staff") that contains, among other important things, a Social Media Policy. The Handbook should communicate that, as a condition of employment or opportunity to volunteer, the Staff is obligated to live committed Christian lifestyles, and this obligation includes the use of social media. And Staff social media postings must be consistent with Church teachings. Therefore, if, in the opinion of church leadership, a Staff member's postings on social media portray images, ideas, or lifestyles inconsistent with Church teachings, then it is grounds for discipline including termination of employment or continued volunteer service.

I'm not an attorney so I recommend you contact David's MG Law Team at TheChurchLawyers.com or other reputable attorney if you have any specific legal questions.

My personal feeling is that you should have the kind
of relationship with your team that would head off
negative social media posting long before it happens.
If you have unhappy employees posting negativity about
your church, ministry, or nonprofit, then you probably
have bigger issues to deal with as a leader.

However, even in extreme situations, the bottom line is that for churches and ministry organizations, there's hope. I wouldn't worry about the occasional comment, but if you're getting employees regularly posting negative comments about your church or ministry on social media, you now have options to pursue.

BLOGGING: PRINCIPLES THAT WORK

In a world that seems to be focused on social media, it's still worth mentioning online blogs, because blogging is as popular as ever. In fact, many bloggers are not only positioning themselves to influence their industry, but making money to boot. If you're interested in blogging as a way of sharing your message or expertise, here are some key principles that will help you find more readers and as a result, have more influence:

Find your niche—what area or issue can you write about that no one else is addressing? In the blogging world, the niche is the new big. Stop trying to address everything and become an expert at a narrow niche. In a clearly defined niche, it's much easier to get noticed and make an impact.

Keep it simple—my blog at PhilCooke.com was tested and is actually written at a 7th grade reading level. At first I was offended, but then I realized it's right on target. Write at a level that's popular, not exclusive. If you prefer to communicate in academic or professional jargon great. That may make you feel intelligent, but you'll reach far fewer readers.

Keep it focused—your readers generally seek it out for one thing. What is your identity? What is your brand? What makes your blog different? Why should I hear from you? What makes you an expert? Whatever people would like to learn from you should be your primary subject.

Keep it short—there's a reason we call people on the web "surfers" and not "readers." Some studies indicate goldfish have longer attention spans. Crazy people on the other hand write forever. Read a typical ransom note and you'll find that it's single spaced, tiny fonts, and no white space. What should that tell you about writing short? (I'm only being partially humorous here.)

Your personal perspective matters. In one case, a housewife simply started writing about raising kids, and now as the kids grew up she developed the site into a mom-housewife-entrepreneur site. She's apparently one of the top blogs in the country and when I first checked in on her years ago she was making about $40,000 a month in advertising. Today it's probably much more. It's all her personal perspective and people love it. (And it doesn't hurt that she's a talented writer.)

Three words: provocative, personal, and preemptive. Be controversial, intimate, and strike before anyone else.

Consider multiple writers. Study The Huffington Post, Church Marketing Sucks, Patheos, and others who use a team of writers, versus my blog that has just me. I love writing, but if you have difficulty doing it regularly, then you might consider getting help—just make sure they are interesting folks who align with your vision.

Are you a creative blog or a content blog? My blog is a creative blog. I write original stuff. I teach. Like it or not, I express my unique voice. But other popular blogs aggregate content from other sources. They don't do anything but scour the web and bring all the articles on a particular issue into one place on a daily basis.

There's always a debate about conflict. Although I wish my serious posts were the most read—sadly, my most popular posts are usually provocative. If I write on the challenges of the new media world, I get readers. But if I would write about a fistfight in a hotel parking lot between pastors, my readership would probably spike. Problem is, I don't want to be the TMZ of religious media, so always think about balance. How you can attract readers and yet still be considered professional.

A blog takes a lot of work and you need to enjoy writing. But if you like to reflect on the issues of the day, have an area of expertise, or love to share your experiences, then it just may be for you. However, the essence of a successful blog is an honest, "behind the scenes," authentic look at your perspective. Whatever your blog is about—theology, pop culture, media, politics—whatever—the first principle is that it's from YOU. It needs to be real, and it needs to be personal. Right now, too many people—especially pastors—are simply hiring someone to cut and paste excerpts from their sermons, books, or other materials into their blog.

Obviously if you're such a big name that people clamor to hear anything you have to say, you'll still get readers. But if not—or if you're trying to build your reputation, brand, platform, or message, then you need to write your comments yourself and they need to be written primarily for the blog. You can tell in a heartbeat those pastors and religious leaders who have blog ghostwriters, editors, or assistants simply pulling other material and inserting it into the blog. It sounds canned, too perfect, and bookish.

Blogs shouldn't be perfect. They should be a little rough around the edges, imprecise, and casual. An interesting blog is really more like an online diary and the people reading it are expecting the kind of thoughts, ideas, and writing they wouldn't find in any of your books or sermons.

Get personal, and get real.

KEY PRINCIPLES TO CONSIDER WITH SOCIAL MEDIA:

1. **The biggest reason people follow you on social media is because they want to know what it's like to be you.** When you reveal the "inside" story of your life via social media, it can encourage, enlighten, and inspire your followers. Posting scripture, positive quotes, and other

things are good, but nothing fascinates your followers like seeing your life "behind the scenes."

2. **Take the time to find your social media voice.** Don't say things on social media you wouldn't say to someone face to face. Use your personality. Talk about the "one big thing" in your life that you're called to do and are passionate about. An important principle is that your "voice" isn't something you make up—it's something you are. Find it and start getting heard.

3. **Use social media to share your faith.** However, it's important to be honest, authentic, relatable, and real. Share your faith on social media in the same way you'd share it with a friend at a coffee shop.

4. **Different platforms have different kinds of followers.** While this isn't always the same across different countries and cultures, leaders (including pastors) generally use Twitter, Facebook is for family and friends, Instagram is visual (and people are moving there in droves), and there are unique audiences for other platforms like WeChat, Weibo, Pinterest, MeetUp, and others. Find the most popular in your country (because they're always changing), learn who's most likely to be using those platforms, and then tailor your message for those different audiences.

5. **When you encounter critics on social media,** never respond in the heat of the moment, and sometimes it's best not to respond at all.

6. **Finally, never forget that social media is *social*.** It's about a conversation, not a one-way message.

— 8 —

PUBLISHING

"History will be kind to me, for I intend to write it."
—Winston Churchill

In the past, writing a book was a massive project. Self-publishing options were few (and usually poor), and to find a traditional publisher was a gamble. But through today's digital technology and on-demand publishing, literally anyone can write a book. A wide range of companies can easily take your manuscript, typeset it, design the cover, and even get the ISBN number and have it listed at amazon.com and other retailers. Our company—Cooke Media Group—has launched a hybrid publishing arm that we believe combines the best of traditional publishers with the best of self-publishing. It's a new model that is changing the way authors look at producing books.

As a result, if you have a message or story worth sharing, there's no reason why you shouldn't consider writing a book. The reason to do it isn't just raging ego, it's getting your story or message down on paper. Before you start thinking writing books isn't for you, these reasons might change your mind:

1. Having a published book supports your perception as an expert. After all, if you're a pastor, executive, teacher, or consultant—having a couple of books to your credit builds credibility. Plus, should you ever leave your current job, you always have your books as solid credentials. While others are waving resumes, you're waving published books. Big difference.

2. It forces you to think through your message. Most leaders go through life with a half-baked idea of what they're really trying to say and do. But the process of writing a book forces you to think it out and express it clearly. It helps give your message substance and structure.

3. It builds your legacy. After all, you've spent a lifetime learning. What are you going to leave behind? Your calling, ideas, and perspectives matter, so consider getting it all down for future readers.

4. Finally—if nothing else, do it for your children and grandchildren. Leave your detailed story so that future generations can know who you are, where you came from, and what you did while you were here. My parents never did that, and now as we comb through their documents after their death, it's a huge challenge trying to sort it all out, and really understand the story of their lives.

Serious writing is tough. But at least the production and distribution of books is easier than ever. You really don't need an agent or traditional publisher. You may not have a best seller on your hands, but at least you wrote it down as a witness and testimony that you were here and made a difference during your lifetime.

THE DIFFERENCE BETWEEN *PASTOR* BOOKS AND *SERIOUS, MORE WEIGHTY* BOOKS

When many pastors and Christian leaders write books, for the most part you can bet most are compiled from sermon notes and manuscripts. Preach a series on fear, and they end up with a book on the subject. Same with marriage, prophecy, grace, Bible stories—whatever. I don't discourage that, but there's a difference in the reader's perception between those books and what readers consider a *serious* book. This isn't a judgment on the quality of your thinking or preaching, it's how the reader perceives different types of books. Writing is different than speaking, and editing sermon notes into a readable manuscript isn't as impressive as a much more extensive literary effort, and here's what I recommend:

1. Go ahead and produce these books I call "pastor books." After all, content should be maximized, and when you preach, that should be available online, through radio and TV, podcasts, and other places—including book form. But understand where these books line up on the food chain. These are books that will mostly help your congregation and other members of your social media or broadcast tribe. These books can often be good, and they are helpful with fundraising, but rarely make a greater impact—*but they do get your message out there.*

2. Next, focus more on your life's great passion or work. Every three to five years, create a book that you pour your life into. Do the deep research, interview expert sources, and do everything you can to make it significant. Sit down and actually write it—don't just preach it (although never waste a potential sermon series). That kind of book deserves serious planning, research, a marketing campaign, and possibly an agent. It should be something you're incredibly proud of and will stand the test of time.

Examples of what I consider "serious" books might be *The Benedict Option* by Rod Dreher, *Boundaries* by Henry Cloud, or the classic *Orthodoxy* by G. K. Chesterton. This was the goal Jonathan Bock and I pursued when we cowrote *The Way Back: How Christians Blew Our Credibility and How We Get It Back.* While these books and others like them could have started as a sermon or teaching series, they needed much more research, depth, and quality of writing to last.

Pastor books are good for teaching, as fundraising premiums, or product offers through your media platforms. The goal of serious books is to stand the test of time. But you'll never write one if you think transcribing a sermon magically becomes a book. If you're serious about your message, at some point you should consider writing more substantial, serious books.

THE TRUTH ABOUT USING A GHOSTWRITER

Today we live in an era of megachurches, major ministries, and global nonprofits. And as bigger churches and ministries grow, the less time their leaders have to actually research and write books—the very products which to a great extent help create their legacy, fund the organization, and put them on the map. Plus, writing well isn't easy. It's a craft and art form just like music, painting, or filmmaking. Writing well takes years of practice and experience, and the discipline to sit for months in front of a computer screen.

That's why many pastors and ministry leaders hire professionals to either assist or do the job for them, which is a perfectly acceptable option. In those cases, there are many levels of working with professional writers.

In my own experience, I have written for clients who gave me original material like sermon transcripts and other notes. In those cases, I was really "adapting" their own thoughts and ideas into book form. In other cases, I literally wrote it from scratch, with little more than a few interviews, a sermon tape, or a conversation or two with the pastor.

But in every case, I never received credit. But that's OK. At least the check cleared.

Is this a problem? Yes and no.

It's usually not a problem because writers are often happy for the work, plus, they offer an important service to leaders. They have certain skills, and like a professional mechanic who fixes your car, or an accountant who keeps your books, some writers are happy to do the work and get a check. They have no desire to be famous, and actually enjoy writing for someone else—after all, it can pay very well.

There's no shame in using a ghostwriter. You're a pastor or ministry leader, not necessarily a professional writer. You may have brilliant content, but not necessarily the skills to get that message down into an engaging book.

On the other hand, it could be a problem because books are far more personal than a car or a checkbook. When someone reads a book, they believe the writing is coming from the heart of the author, and the writing style, the content, and the message reflect the name on the cover. This is true especially in the Christian world, where the message is often a spiritual message conveying eternal truth.

That's why at some level, when a pastor or ministry leader publishes a book with only his name on it, he is making an unstated promise to the reader that the material is his, it's coming directly from his heart and mind, and he's personally presenting it in the form of this book. That's why when possible, I recommend accurate credit on the book cover.

Is it wrong to hire a professional to help you write a book? Absolutely not.

Real professionals can take an anointed message from a man or woman of God and translate it into an exciting and enjoyable reading experience. It's perfectly fine to hire a ghostwriter to help craft your message into a best-selling book. But I would encourage you to at least consider adding the writer's name after yours—even in smaller letters, or with the word "with" before the name.

Possibly the best rule of thumb is the expertise of the ghostwriter. Some writers are simply "hired guns" who can write on any subject. In those cases, I'm more willing to not acknowledge them on the cover, since they're mostly concerned with translating your ideas. Others actually bring past experience and expertise to the table, and in those cases they contribute their own ideas, so I'm more likely to recommend including their name.

Either way—make sure you agree ahead of time so your expectations are the same.

LET'S GIVE GHOSTWRITERS THEIR DUE

Hiring writers, singers, and other artists without giving them credit has been around a long time. Amanda Foreman writing in the *Wall Street Journal* said,

Hollywood had no compunction about substituting soprano Marni Nixon's voice for Marilyn Monroe's for some of the tricky high notes in the movie *Gentlemen Prefer Blondes*. Nixon went on to "voice" Deborah Kerr in *The King and I,* Natalie Wood in *West Side Story* and Audrey Hepburn in *My Fair Lady*—all without studio credit—resulting in her crowning by *TIME* magazine as the "Ghost-ess with the Mostess."

Of course, movie studios aren't the only ones with a history of peddling images over reality. For decades after George Washington's death, his friends and admirers tried to keep the real authorship of his 1796 Farewell Address secret: Washington had supplied the ideas, but Alexander Hamilton's prose had enraptured the public. Two centuries later, John F. Kennedy walked off with the 1957 Pulitzer Prize in history for *Profiles in Courage,* even though most of the chapters were drafted by his gifted speechwriter, Ted Sorensen.

Did you get that? John F. Kennedy took home the Pulitzer Prize for his book *Profiles in Courage,* but a significant contributor wasn't even mentioned.

The issue is especially frustrating in the church where we should be held to a higher standard. The real problem with recent plagiarism revelations surrounding high profile pastors isn't so much the possibility of citation mistakes, but the issue of celebrity pastors taking credit for work they didn't do by themselves. And yet, most celebrity pastors and ministry leaders don't write their books, and still get credit as sole author. After all, that feeds the Christian publishing celebrity machine.

> Bad preachers don't hire professional actors to deliver their sermons. Even when it's your content, you should think twice about taking all the credit for writing a book when someone else is actually doing the writing.

Do secular authors do it? Of course, but who cares? Because we answer to a higher calling—a calling of honesty, integrity, and respect for the people God has given us to lead. Plus, I believe it's also contributed to the "celebrity" culture of Christian leaders today. They've become so well marketed, most people assume they can do anything, and do it all at the level of a superstar.

Don't hesitate to seek the help of a professional writer if you need help because of your schedule, or your difficulty writing well. On the other hand, don't fake it. When appropriate, give the writer a little credit, and let's do our part to keep the perception of the church real and authentic.

In the *Wall Street Journal*, Amanda Foreman went on to say, "In 1949, the Supreme Court ruled that ghostwritten speeches and documents could not be used as evidence in court. The justices deplored 'the custom of putting up decoy authors to impress the guileless.' In short, they weren't going to be taken for rubes, and neither should anyone else."

And most of all, neither should the Church.

E-BOOKS ARE GOOD (FOR SOME THINGS)

I have tablets and e-Readers and I've downloaded about thirty-five books and hundreds of magazine articles to my devices and I love it. It's convenient, easy to carry, and not bad to read. But am I ready to dump real books? Not hardly. If you've ever found an old book at a garage sale, and recognized it as one you'd read years ago—perhaps as a child, you'll know what I mean. There's something about the feel, the smell, and the whole tactile experience of owning physical books.

I can pull many of mine from the shelf and tell you where I wrote notes or what part of the page a certain quote is on. I remember as a young kid reading my first tragedy. It was called *Sabre Jet Ace*—about an Air Force pilot during the Korean War. He became a test pilot, and in the last chapter his engine malfunctioned, he crashed, and was killed. I'll never forget reading it in elementary school. I had yet to read a story where the hero actually died, and I sat there stunned. I kept rereading the last chapter just to make sure it was true. It was such a profound memory that as an adult I spent years searching for that book, and decades later, I found it. Just holding it my hand today brings back that shocked feeling I had as a kid reading the story.

Will e-books do that? I don't know, but I doubt the experience will be the same. Which is why when it comes to books that matter, I'm sticking with paper.

KEY PRINCIPLES TO CONSIDER FOR PUBLISHING:

1. **A printed book can impact your perception as an expert.** While others are waving resumes or giving out copies of sermons, you're sharing published books. Big difference.

2. **A printed book forces you to think through your message.** The process of writing a book forces you to develop your subject and express it clearly. It helps give your message structure.

3. **A printed book builds your legacy.** What are you going to leave behind? Your ideas and perspectives matter, so get it all down for future readers. Leave your detailed story so that future generations can know who you are, where you came from, and what you did while you were here.

4. **If you're not a great writer, there's no shame in working with a ghostwriter.** Find a strong writer with talent and partner with them. The important thing is to get your story down in the most readable and compelling way possible and be willing to share the credit.

5. **Always publish e-books as well as printed books whenever possible.** The race for publishing dominance between printed books and e-books goes back and forth year after year. That tells me the public enjoys both options.

— 9 —

VIDEO, DIGITAL, AND STREAMING MEDIA

"The play button is the most compelling call to action on the web."

—Michael Litt

There's a great deal of buzz about short videos these days, and there are good reasons. Today, more video content is uploaded in thirty days than all three major U.S. TV networks combined have created in thirty years. If your church, ministry, or nonprofit isn't producing short videos regularly, then you're missing an enormous opportunity to share your story with a growing audience. Here are some key reasons why you should consider getting in front of a video camera:

The online audience for short films is enormous and still growing. Research continues to reveal growing audiences are watching. As far back as 2012, ComScore reported the average viewer watched nearly twenty-two hours of video in a single month, and that percentage has been climbing with no sign of letting up. Those viewing hours were broken into many short videos, with each being viewed for just a few minutes at a time.

Audience rating services report that the most influential celebrities in Hollywood are now YouTube stars— often shooting short videos in places like a spare bedroom or their parent's basement.

Nearly anyone can do it. With short videos, authenticity is important, so if you have a mobile phone, then you're ready to go. A higher quality camera is always better, but don't let that keep you from starting. Back when I began working in the industry, you needed hundreds of thousands of dollars for cameras, recording equipment, and lighting. But now, the barrier to entry is so low that chances are, you already own most of the equipment you need to get started.

It's easy to share. Once you've produced a video (I suggest two to four minutes), then you can post it to YouTube, Vimeo, or social media platforms where it can be viewed and shared by your friends and followers. You can use them on your website, blog, or simply e-mail to friends. Speaking of e-mail, according to Forrester Research, including video in an e-mail leads to a whopping 200-300 percent increase in click-through rate. (Think about that when it comes to fundraising.)

And here are a handful of stats that make it even better:

-> 92 percent of mobile video consumers share videos with others, according to Invodo.

-> 46 percent of users take some sort of action after viewing a video ad, according to Online Publishers Association.

-> After watching a video, 64 percent of users are more likely to buy a product online, according to ComScore.

-> According to *Forbes*, 59 percent of executives would rather watch video than read text.

-> 50 percent of executives look for more information after seeing a product/service in a video, according to *Forbes*.

WITH VIDEO, THINK SHORT

In the early days of online videos, research indicated that more than 66 percent of online video viewers turned it off at the two-minute mark. With the growth of mobile devices, and consumers getting more used to viewing on those devices, that has extended to as much as seven minutes. For a captive audience at a live event, banquet, or other presentation—fine, you can go longer. But when it comes to an online video—keep it short. But I continue to see more and more corporate videos, donor development presentations, and promotional video projects at ten, fifteen minutes, or longer. When I ask "Why?" I get the same old answer: "We just had so much information to share."

But what's the point of adding that much information (and length) if people won't watch? Which brings me to the next important issue for producers:

Print is about information. Video is about emotion.

If you want to clobber your audience with the sheer weight of numbers like mission results, fundraising numbers, how many people you're feeding, or outreach statistics, then write it up in written form and hand it out or put it on the website. They can read at their convenience.

But when it comes to a video audience, they'll always connect better through meaning and emotion. Inspire them, don't just inform them.

In the *Wall Street Journal* recently, columnist Peggy Noonan said something similar about political speeches:

> Politicians give 54-minute speeches when they don't know what they're trying to say but are sure the next sentence will tell them. So they keep talking. They keep saying sentences in the hope that meaning will finally emerge from one of them. A 54-minute speech is not a sign of Fidel-like confidence, or a love for speaking. A 54-minute speech is a sign of desperation.

She went on to describe a particular speech by a former politician:

It was a speech about everything—renewable energy, tax credits, Abraham Lincoln, tax loopholes, deficit imbalances, infrastructure, research and development incentives. But a speech about everything is a speech about nothing. I listened once and read it twice: It wasn't a case for reelection, it was a wordage dump.

An effective online video—like a political speech—is not a "wordage dump." It's about meaning. It's about moving your audience toward action.

Short films and online videos can be one of the most effective ways to connect with an audience. But next time, keep it moving, give it meaning, and keep it short. Short video presentations have become one of the most important marketing tools in the world, and there's no better place for using video than sharing our faith.

Evangelism, missions, discipleship, promotions, fundraising—all can be more effective by using short videos. The problem is—most short videos fail. They don't move the audience, call them to action, or motivate.

I was shooting videos and short films back in the days of half-inch black and white reel-to-reel recording. Since that time I've written, directed, and produced at least a thousand videos, commercials, and television programs for a long list of projects and clients. During that time I've learned a few things about producing videos that connect with audiences and inspire them to action. Here's a list of key secrets worth sharing with your communication or media team:

1. A great short film is about emotion, not facts. It's about telling a compelling story, and you don't do that with facts or figures. Instead of boring statistics, I'd rather see the story of one person whose life was transformed because of your ministry. Always think about the emotional angle if you want people to respond.

2. Become a great interviewer. Most of your video presentations will involve interviews, so learn how to put people at ease, make them comfortable, and get honest, authentic answers. Make sure your crew isn't distracting.

Particularly if the interview is about a sensitive subject, make the location a safe place in order to win the person's trust.

3. Watch other short films and videos. Find churches or ministries that do videos well and learn what current styles look like. Stay with the times. Stay up on shooting and editing techniques. Nothing is worse than a video or short film that looks like it was shot ten years ago.

4. It all starts with the script. Whether it's a dramatic or documentary presentation, the writing is more important than anything. As the old Broadway saying goes: *"If it ain't on the page, it ain't on the stage."* Great acting, lighting, or directing can't overcome a bad script. Start with the right words on the page, and the rest will be much easier. Even if the video is improvised, you need to make good notes, and get your ideas down on paper. It will have a huge impact on your ability to tell a story.

5. Never use two things: Cheesy stock footage, and cheap music libraries. Both are deadly. Cheesy stock footage isn't real. It's staged (thumbs up everyone!) and undercuts the reality and importance of your ideas. Bad library music is the same—it stands out, distracts, and turns people away. Take the time to get good shots and find the right music that sets the scene.

6. Lighting matters! I see reality all day long, but when I watch a video presentation, I want to see your vision. Create an artistic world that's fascinating and intriguing. And when it comes to lighting, shadows matter, because what you don't show is just as important as what you show.

With current technology, there's nothing keeping you back from making the best short videos possible. But the best camera in the world in the hands of an amateur won't make much of an impact. That's why building a strong communication team is so important.

HOW TO IMPROVE YOUR CHURCH YOUTUBE CHANNEL

There's no question that a great number of churches and ministry organizations should be addressing today's "digital mission field." And one of the key platforms is YouTube. Most churches and ministries just think YouTube is for randomly posting short video clips of the pastor's message or scenes from the latest mission trip. I asked my friend and YouTube expert Sean Cannell, to give us some examples of how churches and ministry groups can use YouTube more effectively. Here's what he said:

> There are some great churches that are using YouTube very well, but I have yet to discover a church that really "gets" YouTube and is strategically creating content specifically for the over one billion unique monthly YouTube visitors. Most churches are like the Starship Enterprise in need of a "Scotty" in the engine room. Their results with YouTube are good, but with a few tweaks they could reach further and do more than ever before. Here are five key ways to improve your church or ministry YouTube channel:
>
> 1. Create a Channel Trailer—YouTube has a feature to auto-play a video trailer on your YouTube channel to everyone who is not subscribed, telling them why they should subscribe to your channel. This is a great way to explain what your church and your church YouTube channel are all about. The act of creating one will help you clarify your content strategy for YouTube.
>
> 2. Speak to the YouTube Audience—Many churches upload sermons, announcements, and other videos to YouTube, but not many directly engage YouTube viewers. One way to do this would be to add an intro to your sermon videos talking directly to the YouTube audience, encouraging them to like, comment, and share the video, and possibly educating them about other resources, like podcasts, sermon notes, or bonus content on your website.
>
> Many churches create video devotional content or quick update videos that they post directly to YouTube as well. Level-up those videos by including a call to action directly to the YouTube audience at the beginning and end of the video. Verbal calls to action will increase your likes, comments, subscribers and shares which will result in more people discovering your content.

3. Create Remarkable Content with the YouTube Community in Mind—There are some great YouTubers like Jeff Bethke who is well known for his viral video, "Why I Hate Religion, But Love Jesus." That video has been viewed over thirty-four million times and has started many conversations about Jesus. Jeff continues to post weekly videos on his YouTube channel teaching biblical principles and creating engaging content.

There are very creative Christians producing great content every day but not many churches have approached YouTube with the same intentionality. What kind of content could you and your church create specifically for the YouTube audience? As Jeff's video demonstrated, the potential reach of our content is huge and it's growing every day.

4. Engage the YouTube Community—The churches using Facebook and Twitter will engage their online audience by responding to comments and @replies and reaching out to their community with advanced twitter search. What if your church did the same thing on YouTube? Answer questions, comment on church members' YouTube channels, and adopt the same mentality that you have for Facebook and Twitter. After all, YouTube is social network too!

5. Embrace YouTube's Features—There are some very cool features on YouTube that you can creatively utilize for your church's channel. YouTube playlists could be used to group sermon series, devotional series and announcements. You can add any video on YouTube to a playlist on your channel, so you could compile answers to common questions about Christianity from trusted leaders into playlists and share that list with your members. Playlists auto play from video to video and offer search and discovery benefits as well.

Annotations allow you to add call out boxes, comment boxes, and links to other YouTube videos or an external website. Many YouTubers use annotations to give calls to action like asking for likes, comments, and subscribers. They are also useful to linking to other content on your YouTube channel at the end of the video.

If your church doesn't have a YouTube channel yet, create one and start publishing awesome content. If you already have a YouTube channel but it has been a "back burner" platform for your church, crank up the heat! YouTube is most powerful yet underrated social network by church leaders. Apply the suggestions above and if you want more tips for crushing it on YouTube I created a free YouTube Series and e-book that you can access at SeanCannell.com.

SHOULD A CHURCH DIVIDE UP ITS VIDEO AND TV DEPARTMENTS?

As you develop a full media ministry, how you set up the media department's workflow becomes more and more significant. The good news is that a growing number of churches are creating digital media on a very high level, including producing short films, live streaming, and even broadcast television. The bad news is that for some reason, they often divide up the departments—usually into the "video team" and the "broadcast team."

The video team does short films, testimony videos, small group resources, and in-service video announcements. The broadcast team on the other hand, focuses on the TV program and/or the live stream. The problem is that when it's divided into two different departments, the most creative people gravitate toward the video team, because they can more easily express their creativity, produce a wider range of projects, and in some cases, just have more fun—usually because they're less supervised or have more flexible deadlines.

As a result, the "broadcast team"—which is helping the pastor create a broadcast television program (and/or live stream) gets the B-team (or fewer people), even though the TV outreach is, in most cases, reaching far more people with the gospel and the message of the church.

When I ask church leaders why they've allowed this division to happen, I usually get the response that it's because the most contemporary and fastest growing media-oriented churches like Hillsong are doing it.

I asked my friend Ben Field, Head of Film and TV for Hillsong Church and Director of Programming for The Hillsong Channel, how they actually do it. Here's his reply:

> The Hillsong Film and TV department was created to serve our local and global church through the vision of our Senior Pastors Brian and Bobbie Houston. That looks like many things these days from in-service media to worship events, conferences, campaigns, promotions, and in recent years a global TV channel. I believe one of the strengths we've had which has enabled us to grow over the years has been a unified team under a unified vision.
>
> As we all grow, the temptation to split teams and create autonomous silos under different leadership presents itself. Sometimes this can sound like a logical option to manage, but I remember someone saying to me in my early years that multiple visions create division and I've certainly seen moments over the years where that had an opportunity to be birthed if we weren't paying attention.
>
> I love the fact that Christ is building His Church and He would use us to be a part of it. We have to never forget that EVERYTHING we do must be in line with that and the vision of the leadership we serve.

That simply means that Ben is the leader of all electronic media at Hillsong, whether it be short videos, the live stream, outside films, or broadcast TV. All of those crews and creative leaders report to him. That's not to say Hillsong is the only viable model, but after working with hundreds of churches and ministries doing all levels of media, I can tell you this: creatives often forget that in a church setting, the task is to use their creative skills in the service of the church's vision—and the point of that spear is the pastor.

As Ben put it, "Everything we do must be in line with the vision of the leadership we serve." By considering the pastor's broadcast ministry a secondary or B-team outreach, you're crippling the greatest potential outreach you can possibly create.

In my experience, there's only one exception to this rule, and that's when the media ministry is an entirely separate legal entity from the church. If the media ministry is funded, budgeted, and legally a different organization than the church and that media ministry has their own employees, then it's impossible to remove that wall. That was more common in years past than it is today.

But otherwise, when it comes to media, my suggestion is to unify the media under a single vision and make that person an experienced and creative media leader, not a non-media person. Today, the role of media (especially TV) for sharing your story is far too important to consider it a secondary outreach. In a media-driven culture, to reach this generation for Christ, the stakes are too high to get it wrong.

LIVE STREAMING

I have to admit that I never expected live streaming church services and other events to explode like it has in the last number of years. It's allowed millions of people to tap into a church experience or ministry event, and opened up vast audiences that would have never considered actually attending a service. In my case, whenever my wife Kathleen and I travel, it doesn't matter where are in the world, on Sunday morning (depending on the time zone) she always opens her laptop and watches our local church online.

However, thousands of pastors are still afraid of live streaming their services, thinking that once they open that door, people will stop attending the services. While that may be true for some people, it's never been a factor with any of the hundreds of churches with which our team has worked.

But for all the criticism pastors have received for live steaming over the years, suddenly in 2020, during the Coronavirus pandemic, those pastors started looking pretty smart. When the church shutdown was mandated, live streaming was the best option. But *how* you live stream the service matters and from your position as a leader, here are a few things to keep in mind:

Consider it just as important as what's happening in your sanctuary. Don't do an online, streaming feed and treat the viewers like second-class citizens. Make sure it's as high quality as you can afford, and make it available and easy to find. Plus, include them in the service. Address the live stream audience just like you address the live congregation, and make them feel comfortable and welcomed. At least one church calls the live stream service "iChurch," and they treat people that watch online just like members of the congregation.

Understand the online experience is different from the live service. In the live service people are sitting with a large group. They can feel the excitement, and it's a visceral, physical experience. But with the online service, people are watching on a small screen, sometimes from across the room. They're also probably distracted. Shoot more close-ups, and if possible, put microphones in the audience. You want the people at home to feel the power of the service.

Finally—talk to the live stream congregation directly. For instance, in many cases, once a pastor explained to the streaming audience how to give online, it literally doubled the financial response. Why they watch doesn't matter as much as how much you welcome them. They can learn, participate in worship, and support you financially. It's time you took your online congregation seriously.

THE POWER OF SCREENS

In spite of the growing popularity of live streaming, many older pastors still have trouble conceiving the idea that watching a live video stream of a church service is really "church." I still get calls from pastors telling me that online church isn't real "ministry." And to be honest, there is a great deal of research that puts excessive time in front of screens in a bad light, including increased loneliness and a sense of isolation, and after growing up with screens, this generation has difficulty reading a room.

But there's a flip side as well. One comment I received from my friend Larry Ross was fascinating. Larry is the founder and CEO of A. Larry Ross Communications and ran the public relations efforts for more than seventy Billy Graham crusades. He shared this interesting observation:

> In addition to the misconception that live streaming will cannibalize attendance, another fallacy is that the salvation response or impact will be less than live in the main sanctuary, but that is not necessarily the case. First, most people in the house, except perhaps attendees in the first six rows, are watching on the large video screens. But that is amplified when viewing remotely. In fact, at virtually every one of the more than seventy Billy Graham crusades for which I was privileged to coordinate media relations and coverage, the percentage response out of the overflow auditorium (people literally coming forward to a Jumbotron screen) was always much higher than in the main arena or stadium.

The impact was greater and seemed more intimate when Mr. Graham's head was twenty feet tall than seeing him in his entirety as a speck on the stage a football field away.

In other words, those in the back of the arena or in overflow rooms who watched an image magnification screen felt a more intimate sense of reality than those up closer to the stage. The point is that video screens have always been more powerful than most of us think. Which means that we're doing a great disservice to the public when we fail to recognize the power of sharing our worship services and messages online. And it's even more significant when you realize with today's technology, any church of any size can live stream their services.

KEYS TO A SUCCESSFUL LIVE STREAM

During the COVID-19 crisis in 2020, I literally monitored hundreds of live stream services. The good news is that during that experience, more and more church leaders finally started taking live streaming seriously. During that time, I made a list of suggestions to help pastors and communication teams. Keep in mind that this was during a time when 100 percent of the congregation was watching online, but chances are, each of the ideas on this list will help you take your live stream worship to a new level:

1. Make it easy to find! I was amazed at the number of churches who barely mentioned the live stream on their website. With a few church sites, I had to go through five or six clicks to actually find it. Now is the time to make the live stream button BIG and prominently positioned on the home page.

2. Give the early viewers something to watch. In my experience, significant numbers of viewers will tune in fifteen to twenty minutes (sometimes more) before it actually starts. Don't make them stare at a countdown clock graphic or blank screen. Start the live stream early and provide an on-camera host or online pastor to prepare them for the service. It's a great time for sharing church announcements, a prayer time, or other ways to strengthen the connection.

3. When the service starts, consider having the pastor begin with a greeting and/or prayer. Do it just for the online viewers, and it will make them feel more a part of the church family.

4. Use graphics! If you have a graphics capability, add scriptures, sermon points, and other notes to help the viewers. Some studies suggest that videos and TV programs that use text graphics help viewers recall significantly more. Fire up your graphics tools and get more helpful information on the screen.

5. Get a proven platform for your live stream. Using Facebook live or YouTube live is great, but don't forget using professional tools like the *Church Online Platform* on your church website that allows you to insert a countdown clock, chat room, response tools, and more.

6. Don't wait until the end to take an offering. You'd be surprised at how many people will leave the stream early, so if you wait until the end, you'll lose a significant number of potential givers. Find a good break earlier in the service, or perhaps during the preservice time to address giving.

7. Make the live stream available 24/7. I'm surprised at the number of streamed services that end when church service ends. Blank screen. Nothing. I'm unable to replay it. The truth is, you'll get more viewers outside the normal service times if you make it available on demand.

8. This is the most important lesson: It's time to consider your online audience a legitimate congregation. From this point on, you should treat your online viewers as a *campus.* That means, if possible, have a pastor for your online viewers and in the chat room, provide them resources, and be more intentional about making them feel welcome. We often forget that there's always a potential audience watching online. Students away at college, business people who travel, families on vacation.

> **Regardless of your theological position**
> **about what a church service should be,**
> **the practical matter is that you're ignoring**
> **a potentially significant number of people**
> **when you don't take your live stream seriously.**

I can't leave the subject of live streaming without saying that as you begin, you may start with only a few viewers. I spoke with a pastor the other day who is dropping the live stream broadcast of his Sunday worship for that very reason. He was frustrated (and probably a little embarrassed) that only eight to ten people were watching, so he felt like it wasn't worth the trouble. But let me tell you why that completely misses the point of a live stream:

> **What if those eight to ten people actually showed up**
> **physically and visited the church on a Sunday?**

The pastor would be thrilled. He would pull out all the stops to make them feel welcome, enjoy the service, and hopefully come back again.

So why aren't we as thrilled when we have eight to ten watching online?

We live in a world today where many people want to start the relationship by watching at a distance. Still more can't physically show up on Sunday due to travel, illness, disability, or something else. Why not make them feel just as welcome as those who actually show up?

Perhaps in a perfect world, everyone would come, be part of the fellowship, worship together, and grow as disciples. But in today's world, the reality is that won't happen. But on the positive side, digital technology has given us incredible tools for welcoming far more into the service than you can ever see from the pulpit.

And who knows where it could grow? I met a pastor in the Midwest who takes his live stream very seriously. As a result, although he has seven hundred in his actual service on Sunday, ten thousand are watching online. During 2020 when churches were shut down because of the Coronavirus, it was a common thing to hear of churches live streaming to three or four times as many people as had ever walked into the actual church.

Don't worry as much about starting small. Every life you touch with the message of Jesus is worth the effort.

KEY PRINCIPLES TO CONSIDER WITH VIDEO, DIGITAL, AND STREAMING MEDIA:

1. **Short video has become one of the most effective and important marketing tools in the world.** This is becoming a "streaming" world, and this generation prefers to watch a video over reading a book. We should be there with the gospel.

2. **A great short film is about emotion, not facts.** If you want to share facts, then print a brochure or put it on your website. Instead of boring statistics, I'd rather see the story of one person whose life was transformed because of your ministry.

3. **Keep your videos short.** I rarely produce anything longer than two to four minutes. Leave the audience wanting more. As a famous opera singer once said, "You need to stop singing before the audience has stopped listening."

4. **Consider live streaming your church service, conference, or other event.** Your live stream audience can learn, participate in worship, and support you financially. It's time you took your online congregation seriously. It will start small, but don't let that discourage you.

5. **Training is very important with video.** Find someone locally who can help train your team so the videos you produce have an impact.

6. **It's time to take your live stream audience seriously.** They are a legitimate congregation, and we should be intentional about engaging them.

7. **Your live stream will support the church financially if you treat them like a "campus."** Welcome them during the service just like you do the in-house congregation, set the cameras to help them see everything clearly, and follow up with that audience.

8. **Create the role of "online pastor" to minister to those who watch or engage via the live stream or social media.** The truth is, this generation considers "online" to be "community," so we should start respecting that and reaching out.

— 10 —

TELEVISION

> "I hate television. I hate it as much as peanuts.
> But I can't stop eating peanuts."
> —Orson Welles

Over the years, I've done my share of criticizing poorly produced Christian television programs, but one of the most disturbing trends in the ministry world today is the disappointing lack of interest in using TV as a tool for impacting culture. Back in the seventies and eighties in particular, men like Billy Graham, Oral Roberts, Rex Humbard, and others reached vast audiences through television. In spite of some later embarrassments that followed, in many ways those years were considered a "golden era" in Christian broadcasting, and gave birth to numerous global television networks.

But a number of high-profile sex and financial scandals helped turn a younger generation of pastors and leaders against the medium—and far too many cheesy, corny, and low budget programs didn't help. While things are dramatically changing, for many church leaders today, much of what they still see on Christian television doesn't interest them. If that's what TV ministry is, they understandably want no part of it.

As a result, many of these pastors have turned to the Internet and mobile apps as evangelistic and discipleship tools—and aren't remotely considering broadcast TV.

But in spite of the phenomenal growth of the Internet and mobile devices, I still believe television will continue to be an important medium for the Church.

Over the last century, radio never eliminated movies, and TV never eliminated radio. Everything finds its level in the media universe. While the number of households watching traditional TV fell by about 1.2 million last year, television still may be the last truly "mass" medium.

The recent and growing demand for TV commercial spots just confirms that statement. After fears of the web stealing ad revenue, TV ad dollars are rising, and that's why (as of this writing) the average cost of a network TV spot has grown 17 percent during the last TV season. Major advertisers are still looking for the largest possible audience, and this has enormous implications for ministry.

The truth is, while there are many people unplugging from traditional TV and gravitating to the web, these facts are important:

Great numbers of those people are simply viewing popular TV programs on their laptop. They may not be using a traditional TV set, but they're still watching "The Voice," "Modern Family," or the NBA playoffs. I sat on a plane recently next to a woman watching a Joyce Meyer program on her iPad. That same message had been featured on broadcast TV a few weeks earlier. While short films on websites like YouTube are extremely popular, a vast and significant audience is simply trading hardware—not looking for different content.

While more and more people are on Facebook, blogs, and various websites, it's a scattered and splintered audience. There are more than six hundred million Facebook members worldwide, but they're not viewing the same content. It's essentially millions of people interacting with millions of different friends.

TV has become the last great American campfire. To reach a concentrated, mass audience, television is still the medium of choice. Even though local satellite and cable systems have many channels, the most popular number only a handful. As a result, TV has become the last great American campfire. One place where an entire nation—and indeed the world—is focused on virtually the same information and entertainment.

In fact, secular media research indicates TV is still the most effective advertising medium. If our goal is culture change, then the size of the audience means that TV still needs to be in the evangelism mix.

The audience still responds. The last generation of Christian TV viewers were incredible financial givers. Their response to media ministries built universities, hospitals, and some of the largest mission outreaches in history. This generation hasn't proven to give at those levels, but if you can engage them with a relevant message, and amplify that message across social media and other platforms, they still may respond—sometimes financially, and sometimes through action.

In today's culture, the visibility of television programs matter. Ask a nonbeliever about a major Christian figure today and chances are, those with TV ministries are the most likely to be named. Joel Osteen, Joyce Meyer, Billy Graham, Brian Houston, Andy Stanley, T. D. Jakes, Jack Graham, Dudley Rutherford, Greg Laurie, and others are known around the world because of their exposure on television. And for most pastors and leaders, it's not about ego, it's about giving the message visibility.

In many cases, churches already have most of the elements in place for a TV program. The Sunday service is happening weekly, the pastor is teaching, and many churches are already filming their services with multiple cameras. It's not a major step from shooting a service for streaming, IMAG screens, or social media, to developing a broadcast TV program.

TV cuts through the barriers. People can slam the door on someone knocking, refuse to listen to someone share the gospel at work, and stay away from church, but you'd be surprised how often people stumble onto a Christian TV program and actually stick around. I've personally seen letters and e-mails from people whose lives have been transformed simply because they clicked on a Christian program and decided to watch.

One man actually checked into a hotel room with the intention of committing suicide. When he sat on the bed, he accidentally sat on the remote. It turned on the TV and a Christian program was playing. He listened long enough to accept Christ, put the gun down, and go back home. I can give you plenty of other stories as well.

I know you can give me lots of reasons churches shouldn't do TV, and there have been plenty of mistakes in the past. And we could certainly stand to see more creativity as well as correct theology when it comes to programming. But the truth is, television is still a powerful medium, and if we'll take the time to understand how it works, and how it connects with an audience, it still can be an important element in sharing our message with today's culture.

What does that mean for ministry?

It means TV isn't dead—either as an entertainment medium or evangelistic tool. If the Church is going to impact the larger culture, then television should be a priority. Obviously, a total evangelistic, advertising, or marketing campaign needs to embrace multiple platforms, but to reach the largest single segment of people, don't leave TV out of your plans.

But remember the lessons from the past. More poorly produced preaching programs or cheap interview shows will only make your message more and more irrelevant. Changing today's culture isn't just about getting on the right platforms—it's about original ideas that capture people's attention.

It's pretty popular these days to bash local churches producing broadcast TV programs. Even megachurches with adequate budgets for media don't escape the criticism. After all, the history of Christian television shows us that a significant number of programs through the years were downright embarrassing, and if anything, drove people away from the faith rather than toward it. But in spite of the mistakes, poor quality, and questionable results of some church efforts, there's a lot to be said for considering a broadcast ministry—even in today's digital world.

WHAT LOCAL TV CAN DO FOR YOUR CHURCH

While broadcast television can be a powerful national platform, many pastors never consider how much a *local* television broadcast can help their church. Many of our clients have both local and national television outreaches. I always look at both broadcasts individually because they have the ability to accomplish different things. In other states beyond your own, viewers will rarely visit your church, so I generally want to move them deeper into your teaching, either through the website, your live stream, books, audio resources, and more.

For the *local* audience, I want to focus the program on driving them to the church.

Time after time, when we design the local television broadcast toward encouraging people to visit the church, we've seen spikes in attendance. After all, a local television program can give people a glimpse into what your church is like, see your activities, and hear your message.

A new local church member is always better than a TV viewer or supporter because they're more immersed in the local church, become part of the community, and engage on a much deeper level.

And as I've mentioned before, if you're already live streaming (particularly with multiple cameras), you're far closer to having a broadcast TV ministry than you think. A local TV broadcast of a church service gives thousands of people in your city who might never think about visiting a window into your church. In a world where people are hesitant to actually show up, it's a fantastic opportunity to break down the walls and give them an inside look at your worship service.

HOW TO POSITION YOURSELF FOR SUCCESS WITH A TV MINISTRY

If you're actually considering producing a broadcast television program based on your church services, or perhaps you have a different idea, let's get serious for a minute. In an ocean of competition on a typical religious or secular channel, how do you cut through the clutter and get the audience's attention? Better yet, how do you get them to respond?

I don't have all the answers, but here's my list. And by the way, let's take it for granted that you have an actual spiritual call to do this, so don't get mad that my list isn't more spiritual. I'm making the assumption that if you're not spiritually mature enough and called to do this, you shouldn't even be reading this list.

1. The message matters. The truth is, 80 percent of TV preachers are teaching a message few even care about. They're answering questions no one is asking, or they aren't scratching where the culture itches. You may not like Joel Osteen, but his message of hope and encouragement touches a chord in millions of people. Likewise, Joyce Meyer's message of how God works in practical, everyday ways connects just as powerfully. It's not about tickling their ears, it's about connecting—sharing a message that strikes a chord and resonates with people.

In their day, Billy Graham had it, Oral Roberts had it, Bishop Fulton Sheen had it, and others had it. The traditional media world is about *what they think* the audience wants to watch. The new media world is about what the audience wants. Learn something from that. It doesn't mean you pander or water down your theology; it means you speak directly to their point of need.

2. What makes you different? In the world of branding, one of our key questions is "What makes you unique?" Once again, 80 percent of preachers do very little that makes them distinctive, and in a media-driven culture, people need that help. In a world with thousands of choices, it's the different choices that stand out. It's not about preaching a different gospel; it's about being uniquely true to your calling. Don't copy others. Be the nail that sticks out of the porch. Be the blade of grass that stands above the others. Be different. That permeates everything you do—look different, present the message differently, think differently, create a different program, and more.

Essentially, that's what branding is all about. Why should I watch your program? To justify my attention, you've got to be different from all the others out there. We live in a culture where we don't have much time, and we have lots of choices. Make it simple for me.

3. Give me a hook. Why should I respond to you or your message? What's in it that makes me want more? Why should I care? There are lots of preachers out there—and some are preaching good messages, but few give me a reason to want more. The old radio and TV serials invented the "cliff-hanger"—leaving the audience in suspense, demanding to know what happens in the next episode. What are you doing that makes the audience want to come back next week? Creativity, cool graphics, and hip clothes are all fine, but they won't matter if you're not sharing a message that hooks the viewer.

If you don't give them a reason to respond, they won't.

4. Unify your branding. The vast majority of TV ministries have no brand at all, much less know how to unify it. Unifying your brand means that every expression of your brand story needs to be expressed throughout everything you do. From the website, set design, architecture, social media, look and feel of the TV program, printed resources, and more, it all needs to tell the visual story of who you are.

Today, if I spread out the brochures, books, websites, social media graphics, and more from a typical church or ministry, it would look like they each came from a different organization. Therefore, they all tell different stories. But when you see anything from Starbucks, Apple, or Nike—it all has a similar visual expression of their brand. Look at everything you do and make sure the brand story of you and/or your ministry is told through it all. It doesn't have to necessarily look the same, but it needs to tell the same story and point to the same place.

5. Raise the bar. By now, most TV preachers reading this will say, "So what? I do all that already." Maybe, but I doubt it. But even if you are, your standards are probably way too low. You need to realize the level of competition out there. In the 1980s just about anybody could succeed on religious TV. Even Ernest Angley had an audience. But today, the competition is like the Olympics on steroids when it comes to finding an audience. It's a tough world out there, so you need to raise the bar in the level of content, differentiation, branding, and the reason they should respond.

WHY TV GRAPHICS CAN MAKE OR BREAK YOUR PROGRAM

We live in a culture today that is used to information overload, and people can handle multiple streams of information at the same time. I'm not arguing that it's a *good* thing, but it's the truth about how most people live today.

Which brings us to the subject of television graphics.

A quick look at most twenty-four-hour news networks will prove my point. Aside from the actual news reporters on the screen, there's a ribbon across the bottom with a list of entirely different stories, stock market updates, sports scores, and weather, all competing for the viewer's attention.

TV graphics are a way of life, and some research indicates that if used well, they can be critically important for understanding your message. So when it comes to your television program, graphics can make a big difference. Here's how your team can maximize your message through graphics:

1. Listen to the program host, preacher, or teacher. From time to time they will drive people to the phone number, sermon point, scripture, or website, and the director or editor must be listening for those comments. Beat them to it, so the graphic appears at the moment he or she refers to it. There are times they may not ask for it directly, but refer to "giving" or "contacting the ministry"—so be sensitive enough to recognize those moments and use the appropriate graphics.

2. The 6-9 Minute Rule. My experience indicates that viewers typically tune in and out of programs about every six to nine minutes. Therefore, we always want them to be able to see the offer or central message, contact the ministry, know the website, etc. At a very minimum, insert the URL and/or phone number at roughly six- to nine-minute increments when appropriate. This is especially true of identifying the pastor or program host. In other words, as new people are tuning in, be sure and remind them who is speaking on the screen.

3. Be sensitive to the content. Don't just insert a phone number, address, or URL anywhere. Make sure it's not a distraction from the content at the moment. You will maximize your response by being sensitive to what's happening on screen. For instance, if the speaker is making an intense point, that's probably not the time to distract the viewer with a graphic.

4. Be careful with graphic clutter. Be simple and clean with your graphics. Don't clutter up the screen with prices, phone numbers, addresses, etc. Think clean design, and focus on simple, easy to read graphics.

5. Think about font size. We don't have to use large graphics, but in my experience the typical religious TV viewers is often older, and younger viewers may be watching via a mobile device where the image is relatively small. Therefore, "readability" is essential. Make sure the graphic is on long enough and is clear enough for your grandmother to read easily. And to be honest, most people are doing multiple things during a television program—eating, reading a magazine, talking with a friend, etc. Make sure anyone from any age group can clearly notice the information.

6. If it's a scripture or key points, write them on the screen. Few people are watching your program with their Bible open, so when you reference a scripture, put it on the screen.

7. Style is important, but response is more important. We want our graphics to reflect contemporary current TV style, but always question the balance between style, readability, and clarity. The typical viewer needs to get out of his or her chair, find a pen, and write down the number. So keep it up long enough for that to happen.

SOME ADVICE FOR THE FEW WHO DECIDE TO GO BIG TIME

You may be asking, "OK—I'll buy in, but can I actually get a response from viewers of my television ministry?" The truth is, for the vast majority of programmers (either churches or ministries) your response will be less than overwhelming—at least at the beginning. It doesn't negate the value of using television as an outreach because your primary goal is to share the gospel with the largest possible audience.

But certainly in the beginning, your social media, website, phone, and other response platforms can most likely be handled by church or ministry staff members, or well trained and trusted volunteers. I often advise our clients that it will take a year or two just for the TV audience to find you. Considering the number of channels available, and 24/7 programming on each, there may be some time before your viewers discover your program (unless of course you have millions of dollars to promote it).

But at some point, as your media ministry grows, you will need to think about serious solutions. Much of the controversy from TV ministries of the past has been poorly handled financial reporting, so you never want to be anything but serious when it comes to the financial support from your viewers and supporters.

Does it seem like you have a lot of research and planning to do before your first show? You do, but the outcome makes your time and effort worthwhile. After all, by setting your organization on the path God created for it, you can end up touching countless lives.

Obviously, in a digital world, how people connect and respond to any media programming will change. I began my career when the only way to connect with a ministry was phone or mail, so they became the building block of major ministries like Billy Graham, Campus Crusade (CRU), and others. Even today we're finding that the most loyal supporters are still often donors who prefer to deal over the phone or through the mail.

I've said this before, but it's worth remembering:

It's not how you want to reach them,
it's how they want to read you.

Make sure you can accept donations through the mail, online, via text, mobile apps—essentially, any way possible. Not to do that means walking away from what could be significant funding. In the same way, be open to how people want to communicate with you.

If you can keep that in mind, then no matter how things change, or how technology evolves, you'll always be ready to partner with people who want to help you change the world.

SHOULD MY TV PROGRAM BE BROADCAST ON A CHRISTIAN OR SECULAR NETWORK?

Sooner or later, I always get that question, so for the answer, I asked a highly respected media buyer, Chris Busch, Founder of LightQuest Media in Tulsa. What is the right place for your religious TV program? His response:

Simply put, there are more viewers on major secular TV stations and networks, but generally the response rate per dollar spent is lower. If evangelism is the objective, then secular TV provides the most reach and the larger percentage of the "unchurched" audience. If the objective is to maximize response or call Christians to action, then this is usually best achieved on Christian media. While you may be preaching to the choir, that choir is more inclined to have a charitable intent toward your ministry. If audience support of the program and the ministry is critical, then the building of a base of support is best started on Christian channels. There are also opportunities to air internationally, with some countries having Christian platforms as well as secular.

Media ministry usually gets funded through
two channels: viewers who become donors
or through a church's outreach budget.

It's not uncommon for a local church to fund their media ministry out of their missions' budget. As I stated before, in a media-driven world, it's time to start thinking of "missions" in *digital* terms as well as *geographic* terms. By population, Facebook is the largest country on the planet, so digital ministry has now become a true missions outreach.

Media ministries without an underlying church base must look to viewers and donors for the support necessary to operate the ministry. For those para-church media ministries, response to the broadcast (called "name acquisition") and conversion of those contacts into consistent donors is a key element to the economic viability of the broadcast.

If a church chooses to underwrite the media outreach from its budget, then response to the program becomes less critical and placement of the programming on secular platforms can make sense because seeking donations isn't as essential to the objectives of the ministry.

GET THE BEST ADVICE

This was a lot of information to cover, and for anyone not familiar with broadcast radio or television, it can be intimidating. For best advice, seek out someone who's been there. If you know a pastor or ministry leader who has been on television, talk to them, and learn from their experience. There are also many qualified Christian producers with an excellent track record, and our team at Cooke Media Group would be happy to help. Launching out into the world of broadcast media, this isn't the time to start without significant preparation.

KEY PRINCIPLES TO CONSIDER ABOUT TELEVISION:

1. **Just because some "TV Evangelists" may have used television poorly, don't let that persuade you against it.** There's a new wave of creative pastors and ministry leaders who are redefining broadcast media ministry.

2. **While having an online presence is important, never forget that television is still a powerful medium that reaches millions of people.** The best communicators understand that media is about "balance." Getting your message on multiple platforms will yield the best results.

3. **Television can be an excellent tool for impacting your community and encouraging people to visit your church.** It's a great opportunity for your community to see what's happening inside your building on Sunday. Use that TV time to not only preach, but invite people to visit your church.

4. **On-screen text graphics enhance the viewers' ability to remember your message.** That's also true with live streaming, so never forget to insert your scriptures, sermon points, and other key information.

5. **While television can showcase your church or ministry to a vast audience, producing a program, negotiating media time, and evaluating the results can be difficult.** It's always best to get the advice of a proven professional or consultant before you start spending money.

— 11 —

LEADING VOLUNTEERS

"Do everything you can to create an amazing, inspiring experience for your volunteers—and you won't regret it."

—Lesley J. Vos

One normally thinks about the need for volunteers when it comes to small churches or ministries. In fact, most pastors dream of a day when they can hire an adequate staff and not be as reliant on those volunteers. But in a multitude of ways, small could be the best thing that could happen to any church or ministry.

I'm sure you've heard the phrase, "small is the new big." Seth Godin wrote a book about it, and it's been the subject of numerous articles. Last year I spoke on the subject at the Christian Media and Arts Conference in Australia. I'm a firm believer that in the digital age, "big" isn't always the best thing. Certainly companies like Amazon seem to be taking over the world, but for most of us, starting small—and even staying there—isn't failure, it can be freedom.

In my own career I started working with a very large organization, and when I was fired at thirty-six years old, my wife Kathleen and I were suddenly forced to restart small. But looking back, restarting small with a desk in a spare bedroom was the greatest thing that could have happened, and it shaped my perspective on business forever.

Just in case you're not sure about the power of "small," here are the reasons I believe being small is the perfect size for today's disrupted digital world:

1. Small doesn't care about your policies and procedures. As an organization grows, personal decisions and relationships take a backseat to official policies and procedures because once the employee handbook becomes the size of a Bible, then things get complicated. A few years ago we consulted with a large nonprofit whose income had dropped 65 percent. When I talked to the head of donor development I asked if that dramatic drop wasn't a red flag shouting that it was time for a change in strategy. His response? "Nope. We created that fundraising policy years ago, and it worked then, so it should work now." Even in the face of failure, he wasn't willing to change course.

2. Small doesn't care about your salary or office. The bigger the organization, the more petty the conflicts. In fact, sometimes office conflicts are vicious, simply because the stakes are so low. Working out of a garage, spare bedroom, or small rented studio keeps things lean and mean, and there's no time for ego to get in the way. When the stakes are high, people care less about perks like the size of their office or whether it has a window, and care more about making a difference.

3. Small doesn't care about obsessive scheduling. When I worked at a large organization, I had to apply for time off—even if it was to run an important errand. The paperwork and approvals were enormous. Years ago, when I helped rebrand one television network I noticed they required their producers to fill out seven different forms before they could check out any video equipment to shoot a story. Contrast that to creative teams where it's not based on *when* or *how* they work, but *what work needs to get done.*

4. Small doesn't care about the organizational chart. Structure is critically important at large organizations. In fact, most of the work of human resources departments are about keeping the organizational chart clear and functioning. But the most creative and productive teams I've worked with rarely mention titles and act like they don't exist. They don't have fixed communication channels because on creative and productive teams you can talk to whoever you need to talk with to get things done.

5. Small doesn't care about obstacles. Small organizations know obstacles exist because it's all small has ever known—but they're not as big a problem because they're expected. They don't worry as much about budgets because they know they'll get it done somehow—which often makes incredible creativity happen. That's not to say budgets don't matter, and I dream of having big budgets. But for a small team, the size of the budget doesn't hold us back.

6. Small doesn't care about regular meetings. I've discovered that the larger the organization, the more often meetings happen. It's a practical issue to make sure a large team is on track. However:

-> Leaders today average thirty-one hours a month in meetings. It's estimated that half of that time is wasted.

-> 73 percent of professionals admit to doing unrelated work in meetings.

-> 39 percent of professionals admit to dozing off in meetings.

-> That's why small teams are perfect for stand-up meetings, meeting on the run, at lunch, and on the move.

7. Finally, small doesn't care about certainty. The bigger the organization, the more that's at risk and they naturally lean toward being absolutely sure before decisions are made. But look at Paul's missionary journey to Macedonia in the New Testament book of Acts Chapter 16: "Paul and his companions traveled throughout the region of Phrygia and Galatia, having been kept by the Holy Spirit from preaching the word in the province of Asia" (v. 6). In other words, they didn't know where they were going, and just responded as doors opened. They weren't as concerned about certainty as they were the mission.

Never feel embarrassed or ashamed about being small. Whatever size church, ministry, nonprofit, or organization you're leading, understand that in the digital age, small can be a huge advantage. It allows you to be nimble, change course quickly, respond faster, and most important—attempt things that make large organizations nervous.

Amazon started with one man at a desk. Never forget that.

HOW TO MAXIMIZE VOLUNTEERS

Now that I've ranted about how small isn't a death sentence, let's start by maximizing our volunteers. When our team works helping churches use media more effectively, one of the biggest obstacles we often face is the church's attitude toward people who are ready to give away their time for free. Some church and media leaders think volunteers are too difficult to train, others think it's a waste of time, and still others don't see the impact a great volunteer team can have—particularly in media and communication. Some have just given up and don't use them at all.

However, no matter how big your organization, you can stretch your resources and impact by bringing on motivated volunteers. I asked Dan Wathen, our executive producer at Cooke Media Group, about it because he's been a church media director and knows just how effective great volunteers can be for an organization. When it comes to creating a great volunteer team, here are Dan's suggestions:

I've always said if you can manage volunteers you can manage any team. Building a volunteer base might be one of the toughest endeavors a media director will encounter on the job. Over my career, here are six tips I've learned that can make a positive difference for you:

Don't be afraid to ask for help. To your surprise, people want to help but they are just waiting on you to ask. You may be thinking, "Come on, Dan, these people work multiple jobs already and may even have a family." This is true, but many times working in media or another area is a welcome hobby which takes their mind off the everyday. As the Bible says, you have not because you ask not, so give it a shot.

Delegate, delegate, delegate. This was the hardest thing for me to learn and took most of my career to understand. I wanted things to be perfect and in return I was adding more stress and work. The biggest problem was that I was withholding an opportunity for a volunteer. The truth is we all need to give up a bit of control and the desire for perfection and see what could happen with others helping us. Yes, there may be a bit more work on the front end but in the long term it can reap big results.

Set measurable expectations. Don't feel apprehensive and think volunteers don't desire benchmarks because they're not being paid. Set manageable expectations such as: call times, task lists, and due dates. I've found creating detailed job descriptions is a priceless way to add value and expectations to any volunteer position. It may seem like overkill to have this for smaller positions but they will appreciate it and so will your pastor or supervisor.

Locate leaders. These are the people who are not only going to support you but also help implement your vision to the other volunteers. "Buy in" happens when fellow volunteers start to understand the reason behind their work. Approach those on your team who have the respect of the team and display the potential to take on more responsibility.

Communicate to your team. Nothing helps the team more than communicating with them on a regular basis. It's been said that "frustration ends when communication begins." This is so true! I've even solved many volunteer issues by bringing them to my volunteer leaders and allowing them to come up with the solution.

If you lead a department in your church, find your replacement. It's natural to want to protect your job but as the song says, let it go! Always be on the lookout for that person with a unique spark who could one day take your job; then start investing into them. You will find it rewarding to duplicate yourself.

HOW A SINGLE VOLUNTEER OR EMPLOYEE CAN DAMAGE YOUR REPUTATION AND BRAND

It's important to say a word on the damage a single rogue volunteer or employee can cause a church or ministry—and before you think it couldn't happen to you, think again. We regularly see stories of how a single person's bad decision can create a firestorm of negative press coverage. And it's not always because of moral failure or integrity issues, I've discovered that it's usually because of being unprepared.

In the last few years, multiple airlines have been embarrassed because one or two gate agents asked passengers to change their clothes into something more appropriate. But once the photos went public, the passengers weren't offensively dressed at all. Perhaps the gate agent was having a bad day, but the PR damage was done.

In one church a well-meaning African-American usher actually wanted to show more diversity to new visitors. She saw that they used mostly black volunteers as ushers, so she sent an e-mail to those volunteers suggesting that this week, they would be using white ushers. Of course, someone misunderstood, leaked the e-mail to the press, and it turned into a potentially explosive situation. She meant well, after all, she was African-American herself and certainly not racist. But once the story was reported, it made the entire church look racist.

Year ago my wife Kathleen and I were visiting a local church, but we got the address wrong and arrived about five minutes after the service started. When we tried to go into the sanctuary the doors were shut and the usher asked us to go to an overflow room. Looking through the glass doors into the sanctuary we could tell that at least 20 percent of the seats were empty and it would be easy to slip in the back during a song. But the volunteer usher wouldn't budge, and we were forced to sit by ourselves in a distant overflow room.

Needless to say, my wife will never visit that church again.

There are hundreds of other stories of well-intentioned employees or volunteers making innocent but serious mistakes, so here are three ways you can help your employees or volunteers excel:

1. **Teach them to offer options.** When a customer, church member, client, or whoever has a problem, make sure your frontline team members have the flexibility to give them options. One size doesn't fit all when it comes to solving customer or church visitor problems. There comes a time when "policies" matter far less than sensitivity and understanding.

2. **Give them some leeway to make visitors or customers happy.** Have you heard of the Ritz Carlton $2,000 rule? Each employee has the freedom to spend up to $2,000 *per incident* to solve problems for customers—without asking a manager. Organizations like Ritz Carlton know that in the long run they will be rewarded with loyalty and that relationships they preserve are worth far more than any individual transaction. And it's proven by the fact that the average Ritz Carlton customer will spend $250,000 with the Ritz over their lifetime.

Obviously if you're the pastor of a small church or lead a small ministry giving employees and volunteers a blank check isn't possible. But giving them some leeway toward helping fix the problem with a new visitor can save you enormous embarrassment and even hundreds of thousands of dollars in legal bills later.

3. **Teach them people skills.** In my experience, the vast majority of customer problems could be solved if the volunteer or employee simply understood how to respect and deal with people. Taking the time to teach those lessons now could save hundreds of thousands of dollars (maybe more) in the long run.

In many situations, with a more sensitive employee, awkward moments can be turned into an incredibly positive story. But in a social media world, a single act of stupidity, disrespect, or rudeness can blow up to a national incident. How you teach your employees to handle a crisis can save your organization's reputation for years to come.

WHAT CHURCH VOLUNTEERS COULD LEARN FROM DISNEYLAND CHARACTERS

The *Travel and Leisure* website recently revealed that there is one phrase characters at Disneyland aren't allowed to say to any guest. The phrase? "I don't know." Apparently, Disney employees are instructed to go to whatever lengths necessary to help the guest find the answers they're looking for, including asking other employees, making calls, checking things personally—whatever it takes. The goal is to keep guests from wandering around the park wasting time looking for what they need.

I immediately thought of all the church visitors who end up wandering around the church simply because volunteer ushers (and sometimes paid employees) don't take the time to find the answers visitors seek. It doesn't matter if it's the location of children's classrooms, adult classes, the sanctuary, where to get a cup of coffee, restrooms, a request for prayer, or anything else, church volunteers should do whatever it takes to help a new visitor get acclimated and find answers.

In today's distracted culture, people start making decisions within four to eight seconds, so every encounter with a new visitor matters. Training your volunteers and staff to engage in a simple, short conversation with a church visitor could make the difference on their decision to keep coming or visit somewhere else.

Teach your team to value every moment.

KEY PRINCIPLES TO CONSIDER FOR RAISING UP GREAT VOLUNTEERS:

1. **Teach your team to delegate.** One of the greatest problems holding young churches or ministries back is the inability of leaders to delegate. Be intentional about helping your team raise up volunteers to help grow every aspect of your church or ministry.

2. **Set measurable expectations.** Too many church leaders hesitate to expect volunteers to perform like employees. However, when they have clear expectations, it gives them goals, and they feel a greater sense of accomplishment.

3. **Seek out volunteer leaders.** You have business leaders and others in your congregation who are capable of volunteering at very high levels of responsibility. Like a sports coach, you should be scouting out volunteers who have the potential to rise within your church or ministry.

4. **Invest in volunteers—big time.** Most leaders fail to engage volunteers successfully because they don't think training or personal mentoring is worth the trouble. But time after time, when I encounter churches with amazing volunteer ministries, it's because they invested in time, training, and motivating their team.

5. **Celebrate your volunteers.** Give them an inspirational name like the "Dream Team," throw regular parties, create events just for them. Make your volunteer team special and you'll find an army of committed, passionate people dedicated to growing your church.

— 12 —

WORKING WITH CONSULTANTS AND VENDORS

"You are surrounded by simple, obvious solutions that can dramatically increase your income, power, influence, and success. The problem is, you just don't see them."

—Jay Abraham

As you expand your impact through media, you'll be dealing with more and more outside designers, media producers, social media, and other consultants. That's a positive thing because it means you're extending your tent, growing your ministry, and are seeking expertise your team may not have. However, there's a persistent rumor out there that consultants are bad, overcharge, or just prolong your problems for a paycheck. While I'm sure there are bad consultants and vendors out there, to use that as an excuse to not engage good ones will only hold you back.

Most leaders really don't understand how outside consultants can make a difference in helping an organization get to the next level. But in the secular arena, "outsourcing" is all the rage—especially in corporate America. The theory behind the practice is worth thinking about:

If there is some aspect of your business that you don't do well, then outsource it to someone who does.

For instance, a corporation that builds computers might not be so strong at strategic planning, or a company that manufactures sports equipment probably doesn't understand marketing and public relations. So they find consultants with expertise in those areas to give them advice, training, and an outside perspective. Could churches, ministries, and nonprofit organizations benefit from the concept?

Absolutely.

Although our mandate for reaching the culture couldn't be simpler, the various ways available to accomplish that mandate couldn't be more complex. Today, churches and ministries routinely use new technology, the media, marketing strategies, leadership training, and other tools to make their outreaches, educational programs, and ministries more effective—and there's simply no way you'll have experts in most of these areas in your church or on your team.

That's why thousands of churches, ministries, and nonprofits around the world use coaches and consultants in particular fields to help them understand and implement their outreaches more effectively. Coaches are available in areas such as Christian education, computer technology, media, web design, social media, strategic planning, leadership, marketing and advertising, and more, and they can make a real difference in raising the level of competence for your staff members, employees, and leaders.

I've seen many churches and ministries, as well as Christian media organizations, use consultants in the *wrong* ways, I created a list of the ten biggest mistakes. Perhaps this will change your thinking about consultants and give you some innovative ideas about how they can positively impact your organization and mission.

Mistake #1—Assume You Don't Need One. I sat next to a corporate management consultant on a flight recently, and he made an interesting statement: "Today, corporate America understands the power of using consultants, and I'm busier than ever. The single most important role a consultant can play is to provide a fresh perspective, and companies are willing to pay me a lot of money to do just that." Leadership expert John Maxwell calls it "fresh eyes." Everyone needs someone from the outside to bring a new perspective, valuable experience, and cutting edge thinking to their situation.

If you're not using outside sources, especially in areas like media production, TV and radio, strategic planning, advertising, marketing, and fundraising, then you're missing an incredible resource of new ideas, principles, and techniques. If the most successful companies in America use consultants, perhaps churches and ministry organizations should consider them as well.

Mistake #2—Don't Check Their Track Record. Use consultants, but make sure you've hired the right one. Ask for a client list and check them out ahead of time. The best consultants have a credible track record, and you can tell from past clients if they have what it takes to impact your church or ministry. Whatever you do, don't just take the consultant's word for it—there are plenty of overrated folks out there. View their demo reel, client list, portfolio, spreadsheets, or other information that documents past successes, and more importantly, call their former clients and ask about their experiences.

I recently had a great compliment paid to me from one of the fastest growing media ministries, when their top administrator called me and said, "We've spent six months looking at everything on Christian television, and every single time we found something we liked, our research team discovered you either produced it, or were connected with it in some way. That's why we want you to help us." That ministry had done their homework.

Mistake #3—Never Give them Access to the Top Person in the Organization. I know a ministry who recently brought in a fundraising consultant, but never gave her access to the ministry leader. In spite of the fact that the consultant was helping write and edit letters, e-mails, magazine articles, and other materials that needed to express the ministry leader's vision and calling, she never had an opportunity to actually meet and talk with him.

Anyone responsible for expressing the pastor or ministry leader's vision through television, radio, print, or the Internet, desperately needs "face time" with the boss. If the pastor, ministry, or corporate leader is too busy or too important to make time for the people who act as his or her gatekeepers to millions of potential partners, viewers, listeners, or followers—then his or her priorities are way out of whack.

Mistake #4—Always have your Middle Managers Evaluate and Criticize the Consultant's Recommendations. If your in-house management team could have solved the problem, you wouldn't have needed to bring in a consultant in the first place. Over and over, I see Christian organizations hire outside experts to help reshape different aspects of ministry outreaches, but they are constantly being micromanaged, evaluated, or critiqued by less-experienced in-house managers.

Leave the consultant or coach alone long enough to produce results! Certainly don't let him take over the ministry, or work without guidelines or supervision. But please don't dilute his or her work by allowing your managers to meddle with it. After all, if the in-house people are such experts, why are you in the fix you're in now?

Mistake #5—Nickel and Dime Your Consultants. Don't hire a consultant and then financially tie his or her hands. Of course you don't have an unlimited bank account, but sit down with your consultant ahead of time, create an appropriate budget, and then let them work inside that framework. Don't nickel and dime them—especially if they're getting results.

The most successful consultants can be expensive—but if they know what they're doing they are worth every penny. In fact, beware of consultants who sell themselves too cheaply. Let the good ones have the tools and resources they need to make your company or ministry successful.

Mistake #6—Be Afraid They'll Take Over. Most consultants work with numerous clients, travel a great deal, set their own hours, and run their own business—what a great life! Why in the world would they want to take over your ministry? One of the most baffling concerns many ministries have is that consultants want to just come in and hijack the ministry. Actually, nothing could be further from the truth.

Some of the best consultants specialize in areas like media, TV or radio production, fundraising, employee training, strategic planning, information technology, etc. They aren't the least bit interested in dealing with personnel issues, correspondence, shipping, or other general ministry areas. Their greatest joy is to be wildly successful in the area they were hired to fix—not hijack your organization.

Mistake #7—Don't Take Them Seriously. I've never understood churches and ministries that hire consultants and then don't listen to them. I think this must come from insecurity, inexperience, or in a few cases—a raging ego.

The best consultants are people who can transform your ministry and take you to the next level. They often come to you after working with some of the most successful churches, ministries, and organizations in America. Not listening to that type of expertise is like a football team never listening to a winning coach. Don't want to listen? Then don't hire them to begin with.

Mistake #8—If They Make a Mistake, Get Rid of Them. I actually like consultants to make mistakes. It means they are trying new things, overreaching, and pushing the limits. Give your consultant room to present ideas you might not like, or don't think would work. Give them a little latitude, and they'll pay you back in spades with creative work, innovative ideas, and most of all—results.

When they do make a mistake or present an idea or project you don't like—don't just dismiss them. Sit down and discuss it at length—what you liked and didn't like, and let them defend their thinking. Very often, the motives and reasons are sound, and have been used successfully elsewhere. Listen, and it might just change your opinion—and your future.

Mistake #9—Don't Recommend Them to Others. A regular joke in the world of consulting is that every client wants to think they're the only client the consultant has. But the more clients your consultant works with, the wider range of experience, data, and ideas he brings to your table. Don't hog a good consultant—after all, we're all on the same team. Help your church and ministry friends by sharing good consultants and expanding their client base. Although good consultants keep their information from other organizations highly confidential, their experiences from other ministries will only help you.

Mistake #10—Only Use Them for Short-Term Projects. In the business world, client-consultant relationships work for years, and even decades. In television production for instance, it might take years to build or reshape your television outreach—especially at a national level. Training a crew, buying the right equipment, selecting the best TV stations and networks, building a fundraising program, developing a long-term media strategy, branding your program, advertising and promotion, graphic design, exploring international media opportunities, and more, take time.

Sometimes a consultant can come in and fix something right away, but that's the exception rather than the rule. Look for a consultant who can provide a long-term plan for helping you achieve your goals, and make sure he has the staff, resources, and tools for staying with you for the long haul, and taking your church or ministry to the far reaches of success and effectiveness.

Never forget the concept of "fresh eyes" and how you could benefit from another perspective. Sometimes, an outside voice can reveal a door that you never realized was available.

HOW TO HAVE AN AMAZING RELATIONSHIP WITH A VENDOR

Personally, I am a consultant to churches and ministries, but our company is also a "vendor." That means our team is hired by churches, ministry organizations, and nonprofits to do more than coach or share ideas; we're often engaged to create or produce a wide range of projects, from video and short film production, social media, book publishing, web design, and more. Essentially we help organizations engage today's digital culture more effectively.

But as a vendor, we sometimes encounter organizations that are unsure how to maximize our relationship. Whenever you hire a coach, consultant, or other type of vendor, it's important to realize that it's a two-way street. To make the relationship work well, here are several things you should know before you hire a consultant or vendor from the outside:

Your own ideas will help. Obviously you have a challenge, and that's why you're hiring an outside vendor or consultant. But share with them any ideas you already have on solving the problem. No matter how inexperienced you may be, your ideas matter and will help the vendor. Plus, hearing your ideas will help the vendor understand what's been tried before and the boundaries he or she will have to work with. Think like a partnership, not a solo act.

Prepare to be challenged. Expect the unexpected. You're hiring outside advice, so don't assume they'll give you what you've already considered. In fact, come ready to put up a fight—not in a nasty way, of course, but know that creative disagreement is often the formula for the most brilliant ideas.

Give him or her some leeway. Give the vendor some creative freedom and encourage them to bring unusual ideas to the table. Besides, if you're only interested in conventional ideas, did you really need to hire them? Especially if the vendor has a strong track record for delivering, let them show you what they can do before you start limiting their options.

Understand the areas where success can't be guaranteed. A consultant or vendor can do the best job possible, but can't guarantee you'll publish a best-selling book, sell out your conference, or hit a fundraising target. Know the difference between areas where performance can be assured and where it can't—even with the best advice and counsel.

Finally, do hold them accountable. I'm amazed at the terrible work some vendors do and are never held accountable. In most cases, it's because the person doing the hiring doesn't hold them to their agreement. In fairness, make sure your team has given the consultant the cooperation and resources to be successful. But work out performance standards ahead of time so your expectations are realistic.

I'm not suggesting legal action (except perhaps in a case of gross or criminal misconduct), but you should expect vendors to accomplish what they promise. If they don't, cut them loose, simple as that.

A good contractor/vendor relationship should be a win for both parties. For a variety of reasons, some relationships don't work out, but if you follow these five principles, you could have a long-term and highly successful relationship.

THE RIGHT POINT PERSON ON A PROJECT IS VITAL

At some point, your organization is going to work with a vendor, consultant, or other outside group, and whenever that happens, there's a crucial issue that too many organizations don't think enough about: *your contact person*. Some call them a "liaison," a "go-between," or "point person." Whatever you call your employee that handles it, that role is critical to your success. Here are a few tips for picking the right person to deal with outside groups:

It shouldn't be the person whose failure is the reason the outsider was brought in. It sounds obvious, but it happens surprisingly often. A nonprofit is unhappy with their inside fundraiser, so they hire an outside donor strategist for some new ideas. But in many cases, they have their inside fundraising person (the one who's failing) be the contact person for the new, outside group.

Really bad idea.

The inside employee is already smarting from their failure, and the last thing they want is to see an outsider excel where they didn't. They'll often undermine the project, and at the very least, throw unreasonable obstacles at the outside group.

I know, I know, no person on your team would ever do that. Really? I can assure you, I've seen it more often than you think.

It should be a relatively high-level person on your team. Depending on the job, the inside employee will be seeing budgets, confidential information, statistics, and other details that you might not want a lower ranking employee to see. Make sure your employee contact is at the same level of leadership, experience, and expertise as your outside coach, vendor, or consultant. I've seen situations where a lower paid employee was the vendor contact, felt the vendor was making or spending too much money, and became resentful. It's all about perspective, and you need someone who has a mature attitude.

It shouldn't be a person who is too opinionated. Sometimes, the contact person let's his or her personal opinion get in the way of an outsider's new ideas. You're paying the outside organization for new thinking, so don't let your own team member undermine it.

Finally, make sure your contact person has good social skills. In any outside relationship there will be misunderstandings, miscues, and innocent mistakes. Your employee should have the people skills to keep everything on a friendly basis, and not panic at the slightest problem. If your contact person is someone who goes hysterical at the smallest issue, they will quickly destroy what could be a long and productive relationship.

You get most of your information about how the project is going from your inside contact. Make sure that they have the experience, people skills, and creativity—plus, are secure enough in their job to manage the kind of relationships that will be successful.

WHY CHURCHES SHOULD APPLY THEIR VISITOR STRATEGY TO VENDORS AND CONTRACTORS

When it comes to new visitors, most church employees are warm and welcoming. They have a strategic plan to make visitors feel at home, are followed up, and get plugged into the local church community. However, when it comes to outside vendors, contractors, freelancers, or consultants, church employees are often skeptical, uninterested, and sometimes outright hostile.

Why the difference?

Churches are often what could be called "self-contained organisms." They don't need much outside input or resources to operate, and as a result, tend to be inward focused instead of *outward* focused. The problem is, that also creates stagnation, because the inside team isn't hearing new ideas and being challenged by those with more expertise. And even when outsiders are hired, typical church employees rarely encounter contractors because that's usually handled by an executive pastor or facilities manager.

That's why I've met so many outside church contractors, A/V consultants, engineers, designers, freelancers, and others with very negative feelings about their experience. It's not so much about job performance, because every contractor or freelancer should be used to meeting high standards. It's more about the typical church employee's inexperience dealing with outsiders, and far too often—employee insecurity about outsiders being there at all.

But outside consultants, contractors, and other vendors can be a powerful witness for the church. They often have many of their own employees who could be potential church members, or in the case of freelancers and consultants, they often have highly regarded reputations and influence that could greatly benefit the church.

Here's a suggestion: Have your church apply your visitor strategy to vendors and contractors. In other words, use the same techniques to engage outside working contractors and vendors that you use for making church visitors welcome. Instead of cultivating an "outsider" mentality which too often results in feelings of competition, insecurity, suspicion, and skepticism—let's create a welcoming and honoring atmosphere where everyone can do amazing work.

It doesn't matter if it's a construction team, a freelance designer, a communications consultant, a marketing firm, an audio or video installer, or someone else. Every day make them feel like a Sunday visitor, and watch your church's impact skyrocket.

KEY PRINCIPLES TO CONSIDER FOR WORKING WITH A CONSULTANT OR VENDOR:

1. When it comes to working with consultants and vendors, don't be afraid to start with your own ideas and suggestions. No matter how inexperienced you may be, your ideas matter and will help the vendor. Think like a partnership, not a solo act.

2. Prepare to be challenged with new ideas and ways of thinking. You're hiring outside advice, so don't assume they'll give you what you've already thought about. It may give you a completely new perspective.

3. Give the vendor some creative freedom and encourage them to bring unusual ideas to the table. Especially if the vendor has a strong track record for delivering, let them show you what they can do before you start limiting their options.

4. Understand the areas where success can't be guaranteed. A consultant or vendor can do the best job possible, but can't guarantee you'll publish a best-selling book, sell out your conference, or hit a fundraising target. Know the difference between areas where performance can be assured and where it can't—even with the best advice and counsel.

5. Make sure the "point person" from your organization who deals with the consultant or vendor is experienced, mature, and professional. If the consultant or vendor is a professional, you'll only hurt the results if you make them work through one of your assistants, or a low-level manager.

— 13 —

FUNDRAISING

"Donors don't give to institutions. They invest in ideas and people in whom they believe."

—G. T. Smith

The U.S. government has given nonprofit status to organizations created to serve the common good. Humanitarian efforts, religious organizations, educational institutions, medical services—all are common types of nonprofit groups. They accept donations, and are exempt from taxation, which allows them enormous financial incentives and latitude. Therefore, in the case of churches and ministries, fundraising has become a vital tool that's used to raise the necessary money to make ministry happen.

However, in many cases, the tail has started to wag the dog.

Today, some ministries have virtually changed their sense of original mission to a primary focus on raising money.

For many pastors and church leaders, it's not a surprise that for many organizations today, fundraising is a massive business. That's not a bad thing, because it's helped great organizations raise billions of dollars to do wonderful work. However, it has spawned financial consultants, direct response companies, fulfillment businesses, capital campaigns, and more. Helping ministries raise money has become an industry in itself.

The encouraging "personal" ministry letter you receive each month is probably not written by the ministry leader at all, but by a direct mail strategist, and it was designed by a graphic designer for maximum response. Today, color scheme, spacing, layout, and structure are some of the most important features of monthly letters and e-mail blasts—and the most effective direct response fundraisers can even compare results based on different colors of the envelope.

Traditionally, they mailed the letter on just the right day each month so it would arrive when people received their paycheck. Statistics proved that if it was only a few days late, the response would drop considerably. I've seen people fired from nonprofits because they mailed the monthly letter forty-eight to seventy-two hours behind schedule—it was considered that important. Today with additional options like online giving and direct deposit, the day of the month the letter is mailed isn't as important, but fundraising experts still take data like that into consideration.

In fact, I spoke to one fundraiser who said that the single most important thing is getting a person to open the envelope—and he would be willing to do pretty much anything to make that happen.

Even lie about what's inside.

Let me be clear: I'm not against fundraising. There are some marvelous ministries and nonprofits out there doing great work because of effective relationships with their supporters and partners. And I work on a daily basis with donor development experts of the highest integrity. But as a pastor or ministry leader who may be unfamiliar with professional fundraising, you need to know how the business works.

I also believe givers should be more informed. As a donor, don't become a ministry zombie and give on impulse—for any reason. Give because you've researched a ministry, believe in what it's accomplishing, have confirmed its integrity and track record, and then prayed about the gift.

Giving for any other reason is usually a waste of money.

And if you're the church or ministry leader, by all means ask for support. Just make sure you have integrity in the way you ask, and in the projects you're launching.

FUNDRAISING METHODS

"Transactional" based fundraising is typical of a young ministry or nonprofit. At first, a young ministry or nonprofit has no real supporters, and they must rely on selling products like books, online teaching resources, or other products to raise money. That's actually a good thing, because I'm really big on getting your teaching materials into people's homes. It's one thing to reach them in the pulpit, online, or on radio or TV. It's something else entirely when they are reading your material at home or listening to your podcast in the car. It takes your influence into their life down to a much deeper level.

The bad news is that it's temporary. The response to transactional ministries is only as good as their last product. And if you don't have a constant pipeline of product, you start to find gaps in your fundraising. Plus, there's very little evidence that indicates people who buy books or other resources, grow into regular supporters on their own. It's a good start, but not really sustainable.

> Development or capital campaigns
> can be good because they do
> a lot of wonderful things in the world.

They build water wells, orphanages, Bible schools, universities, and more. Sadly there are still way too many fundraising campaigns built around prosperity, financial "blessing," and dodgy stuff like numerology (I passed seven stoplights on the way to the studio today, and felt God tell me that when you give a financial gift of $70, you'll receive your miracle).

But if we can keep doing great work out there,
I'm all for campaigns. The problem is that
if you're not consistent, it can confuse your branding.

For instance, if you're doing water wells one month, building a Bible school the next, and inner-city ministry the next, the audience begins to wonder who you are and what your real calling is. The key is "What is the overarching calling of your life and ministry?" If you can answer that, then it becomes a brand umbrella with your campaigns and good works coming under it and following that theme. But without that focus (or brand), your appeals become disjointed to the supporter, who finds it impossible to decide who you are and what your ministry is really about.

Partnership is the holy grail of fundraising.

Transaction based giving is a good place to start, but long term, giving through *partnership* is better. Partnership happens when your work is so compelling that people join you—not for a book, product, or a single campaign—but because of who you are and what you do. They believe in your ministry purpose. They understand your calling, see clearly what you're all about, and want to join up and be a part of what you're doing in the world. They don't need a book or other gift in exchange for their donation. As a result, real "partners" give on a regular monthly basis, and have a much longer term vision for their relationship to your ministry.

But partnership must be developed and nurtured, and you have to be reporting the results of your work to the supporters. Long experience has taught me that if you don't photograph or film your work to show your supporters, it doesn't exist in their minds. Back in the day, Oral Roberts and Billy Graham kept detailed index cards of every person that accepted Christ at their crusades. I've personally read through hundreds of Oral's cards and it's a fascinating experience. They didn't do it because of ego. It was because they knew the importance of quantifying the results of the mission.

Without results, you can't go back
to the well for more support.

And just in case you feel uncomfortable asking for support, it may sound noble, but the fact is, there are probably people out there who would like to help you accomplish your work. But by not asking them, you're denying them that opportunity. I really don't personally believe there's any nobility in not asking for money. If you're a church, ministry, or nonprofit, you exist because enough people are willing to support your work. But unless you ask, how will they know about what you're doing?

It doesn't have to be done in an awkward or cheesy way. Just ask.

CREATIVITY MATTERS TO DONORS

A great number of nonprofit organizations and Christian ministries do remarkable work, but do a poor job of telling their story. It's not really so surprising, because after all, they're experts at doing the work, not talking about it. But more and more proof is coming in that donors are looking to be engaged with your work. Therefore, when you don't tell your story well, you could be losing more than a third of your potential donors.

My friends and fundraising experts at Dunham+Company alerted us to a study from Abila Research that indicates "Nearly three-quarters (72 percent) of donors say poor content affects whether they decide to donate to a nonprofit organization." Because of the overwhelming media clutter out there, we have to be more innovative than ever to reach audiences and make an impact today. Says Jennifer Abohosh, Senior Digital Strategist at Dunham+Company, "This study confirms what we know to be true: content is king. But when it comes to donors, that content must be relevant in order to keep them engaged."

Whatever we do—online videos, radio and TV, podcasts, social media, our web presence, print media—all have to be more creative than ever in order to cut through the clutter and get noticed. Plus—when it comes to fundraising and donor development, if we're not telling compelling stories about the impact we're making, then it's as if it never happened. Donors need to know about your work, and the lives you're changing.

> *How* we share our message is just as
> important as the message we share.

Very often in ministry, "creativity" gets the short end of the budget. But we need to invest in our creative teams, and our strategy for breaking through and getting a response.

THE POWER OF VIDEO FOR FUNDRAISING

In a previous chapter we discussed the growth and popularity of short videos, and today, hundreds of nonprofit organizations and religious ministries use fundraising videos to tell their story. It's a powerful medium, and along with other projects, our team produces fundraising and donor development videos for some of the largest nonprofits and ministries in the country. After years of producing these projects around the world, we've discovered some important keys to creating an impact with the audience. The next time your organization considers a promotional or donor video for your website, social media, or to show at a live event, here are some important principles:

Keep it short. For a live presentation you have a captive audience, but even then I rarely produce anything longer than four to six minutes at the most. Leave the audience wanting more.

A successful fundraising video isn't about facts, it's about emotion. The audience won't be moved by the fact that last year you served ten thousand meals, housed five hundred homeless people, or built a medical clinic in the Congo. They want to see the lives changed because of what you did. Stop using statistics with fancy graphics and start telling stories. If you need to share facts, then print them on a brochure or put them on your website.

Don't create a music video. I don't care how much that popular new worship song means to you, illustrating a song with shots of your work doesn't impress anybody. Interview people and let them tell the story, or have a narrator do it. Music videos rarely lend themselves to sharing your vision, showing the results, and calling people to action.

Do it well. Your brother-in-law may have a home video camera, but he's not going to show the emotion, the drama, or the story an experienced professional will capture. The point of a donor development video is to call the viewer to action, so get the kind of advice you need to do it well. I can't stress enough the potential of a compelling video presentation, so don't leave it to chance. Be creative, be contemporary, and most of all, be strategic.

Potential donors want to hear your story, and in today's visual culture, showing a powerful video is an incredible tool. The question is: What's the message or story your organization needs to tell?

WHAT ARE YOU FIGHTING?

When it comes to your ministry or nonprofit organization, like it or not, an important aspect of successful fundraising is that it needs an enemy. Sometimes that enemy is hunger. Sometimes that enemy is drug addiction, alcoholism, or child abuse. It could be spiritual darkness. It shouldn't be individuals, but it can be a group such as drug dealers, human traffickers, child predators, etc. The questions you need to think about are:

What are you fighting?

What are the people you're talking to passionate about?

When you can figure that out, you have the potential key to getting your audience to pick up the phone or go online and help you make a difference. Identifying an enemy is a powerful way to motivate support.

DO DONORS LIKE E-MAIL OR SNAIL MAIL?

You've probably had someone on your team tell you that direct mail is over as a fundraising tool. Certainly there's a transition happening, but research indicates that most donors see advantages to both e-mail and direct mail communication from the organizations they support, and one study reveals that very few completely reject one form or the other. The study of one thousand American charitable donors shows that very few donors consistently see e-mail or direct mail as a better way for nonprofit organizations to communicate with them. The Donor Mindset Study, conducted jointly by Grey Matter Research (Phoenix, AZ) and Opinions 4 Good (Op4G, Portsmouth, NH), asked donors to compare the two methods of communication from organizations they already support on six different factors. Which method is:

-> *more likely to get read*

-> *more likely to be discard unopened*

-> *a better use of the organization's resources*

-> *more likely to annoy them*

-> *more effective at communicating facts and information*

-> *more effective at telling a touching story*

When it comes to which method is more likely to be read, donors are almost evenly divided—37 percent feel they are more likely to read direct mail, 35 percent e-mail, and 28 percent say they're equally likely to read each one. Age plays a role in this, but not a big one. Among donors under age thirty-five, e-mail from charitable organizations is more likely than direct mail to get read, but only by a 44 percent to 35 percent margin. Among donors sixty-five and older, direct mail wins by a relatively small margin, 39 percent to 29 percent.

The two methods may be equally likely to get read, but donors do find it easier to discard direct mail unopened (41 percent, compared to 26 percent for e-mail). This may be because the carrier envelope acts as a "preview" for direct mail, allowing donors to see the purpose of the mailing, while some people may have to open the e-mail in order to see what it's all about.

Reading some communications and tossing others away unopened are not mutually exclusive activities. Thirty-four percent of those who are more likely to read direct mail are also more likely to discard it unopened; for e-mail, that figure is 20 percent. In fact, only 21 percent of donors are truly biased toward e-mail, as they're both more likely to read it and more likely to discard direct mail unopened. Almost as many (16 percent) are truly biased toward direct mail in the same manner. Most donors simply do not have strong preferences in how the charitable organizations they support choose to communicate with them.

Donors do have the feeling that direct mail is more effective at communicating with them. Direct mail has only a slight perceptual advantage at communicating facts and information (37 percent to 32 percent), but it has a substantial advantage at telling a touching story (38 percent to 23 percent). Even among the youngest donors, who are often assumed to reject direct mail in favor of digital communication, 38 percent give direct mail the advantage at telling stories (versus 35 percent for e-mail). Among donors sixty-five and older, the perception is strongly in favor of direct mail (47 percent, to just 13 percent for e-mail).

Where e-mail has an advantage is in not annoying donors—but it's only a slight advantage. Twenty-eight percent say they are more likely to be annoyed by receiving e-mail from an organization they support, while 34 percent are more likely to be annoyed by direct mail. Younger donors are the ones more likely to be annoyed by direct mail than by e-mail (45 percent to 24 percent), while among donors thirty-five and older it's evenly split between the two.

Where e-mail has a substantial advantage is in the perception that it is a better use of an organization's resources. Fifty-five percent of all donors feel this way, while 24 percent believe direct mail is a better use of resources. This is one perception that does not vary by age group.

Ron Sellers, president of Grey Matter Research, notes that this study may help combat some common myths about donor communications.

"There are some in the industry who preach that older donors simply won't accept digital communication, or that young donors reject traditional direct mail," Sellers said. "While different ages do lean toward one method or the other, most donors are quite accepting of both methods." He explained that only 4 percent of all donors feel direct mail is superior to e-mail on all six of these measured factors, while just 6 percent rate e-mail as superior on all six. The vast majority see advantages to both methods.

Sellers pointed out that when new methods are introduced, there's often a rush to "bury" traditional methods, but what frequently happens is that consumers get used to having more choices rather than migrating quickly from the traditional to the new. "We heard that with the introduction of online and mobile banking, bank branches would be closing all over the country—yet there are more branches in the U.S. today than in 2007. We heard that with the increased number of television channels, the big networks would quickly die—yet they're still very much alive. We've also heard many times that direct mail is dead and that e-mail is how nonprofits should be communicating with donors. The reality is that donors usually accept both. Just like with banking and TV, they get used to having more options."

THE IMPORTANCE OF THE OLDER GENERATION FOR FUNDRAISING

Everybody wants to reach "the next generation," and I can understand that. When nonprofits come to us for help, they want to focus on the twenty-something crowd, and make sure their website is hip and cool and appeals to younger people. But the brutal truth is—when it comes to fundraising, older folks still carry the load. Pop music belongs to the young, giving belongs to the old. That's not to say we should turn off younger people, but don't be fooled by the illusion that they will necessarily support your cause in a significant financial way.

People will reply: "What about the massive amount of money that was raised through text messaging by young people after the Haiti earthquake?"

That's a good point, but where is it now? Young people are largely impulse givers. They see an appeal, get emotional, and text a $10 gift. But soon after, they're off to the next big thing. It's the older crowd that continues to give for the long term. The millions that were quickly raised for Haiti or the Live Aid concerts are really peanuts compared to the long-term, sustainable giving that age fifty and older people do on a daily basis.

The bottom line is to focus on the older audience if you need to raise serious money.

By the way—that doesn't mean your TV, radio, or web campaigns have to be traditional or stodgy. Even old people want to be cool. But focus it on their interests, their values, and their goals.

Your chances of success will be much greater. My advice? Raise *money* from the older audience, but raise your *perception* with the young. After all, they'll be the next generation of givers.

KEY PRINCIPLES TO CONSIDER ABOUT FUNDRAISING:

1. **Fundraising isn't about asking for money as much as it is about presenting your vision and giving people the opportunity to support that vision financially.** Which means that just because other organizations do fundraising poorly, don't let that deter you from giving people the chance to help you accomplish your goals.

2. **Fundraising can be easily manipulated, which is why it's very important that you maintain integrity and credibility.** Getting the advice of reputable donor development advisors or consultants is vital.

3. **It's not just about how *you* want to reach *them*, it's also about how *they* want to reach *you*.** Some people respond to snail mail, others to e-mail, and still others to online giving or apps. One isn't better than the others; it's all about what your congregation, followers, or donors are most comfortable using.

4. **What are you fighting?** A cause is a powerful reason people will get onboard and take action.

5. **In your determination to reach a younger generation, never forget that older people are still the most financially secure and therefore able to give.** That cycle is always changing as people get older, but don't forget that an older audience can really help you achieve your goals. That doesn't mean you only have to do things for that generation, but present your cause in a way that will excite them, and you'll reach that goal earlier.

— 14 —

HANDLING A CRISIS

"It takes twenty years to build a reputation and five minutes to ruin it. If you think about that, you'll do things differently."

—Warren Buffet

Good public relations isn't just about promoting the great things you do. In many cases today it's about managing criticism, negative publicity, or outright wrongdoing. But in my experience, the vast majority of pastors and ministry leaders don't think disaster could ever strike. They feel as long as they stay focused on God and lead their church well, they can avoid bad publicity or some other crisis. But the truth is, bad stuff happens—and often, it's absolutely nothing you can predict or control. Just in my career working with churches and ministry leaders, here's a representative handful of crises I've seen that no one expected:

-> A trusted church staff member was caught embezzling tens of thousands of dollars out of the church bank account.

-> A long time usher was pocketing cash out of the offering while he was supposed to be counting it. Over a couple of years, it added up to a great deal.

-> A much older pastoral staff member was arrested for having an online relationship with a minor. What he didn't know was what he "thought" was a minor, was actually a police detective. He was arrested as a pedophile on his way to a rendezvous.

-> A mission organization a church had supported turned out to be abusing orphans in their care.

-> A ministry leader's son had a temper problem and was arrested after beating up an employee.

-> A pastor had an affair.

-> A church staff member recruited members of the congregation for an investment scheme that turned out to be a scam. Many church members were financially wiped out and sued the church.

-> . . . the list goes on and on. Disaster can happen. Actually, you should plan that a disaster *will* happen. In today's litigious world, you can't be too careful.

DON'T WAIT UNTIL A CRISIS HAPPENS

Sir Jonathan Miller is a highly regarded theatrical director based in London, and while I was watching him work on a BBC documentary, he said something simple but brilliant: "You learn to ice skate in the summertime." He mentioned it was a lesson his father taught him. It took some time for it to sink in, and then I realized the power of what he was really saying. Once the game, project, production, business, crisis—whatever starts, it's too late to learn what to do. Take the classes, learn the techniques, get the knowledge before the crisis begins, or you'll be behind once it happens.

It's been said that good generals plan for battle, but great generals plan for the unexpected. What are you doing right now that will prepare you for when your great crisis—or great opportunity—happens?

THE DONNER PARTY AND HOW TO DEAL WITH A CRISIS

One of my favorite places in the world is Donner Lake, California. Less than ten miles from the much larger Lake Tahoe, it's the location where the famous Donner Party—a group of California-bound settlers—were snowbound in the Sierra Nevada Mountains during the winter of 1846–1847. It was a record snowfall, and survival became so perilous, some of the travelers resorted to cannibalism. They had arrived at the Donner Lake area just before the winter snowfall became heavy, and the group debated on moving forward versus waiting it out.

The group that wanted to wait it out won the day, and a great tragedy resulted. While I'm all for strategy, serious reflection, and thinking, I believe I would have voted to keep moving. Sitting still is very difficult for me, and I'm not one to wait anything out without a clear reason.

When it comes to leading organizations, as I think about going through a crisis of any kind, I have to decide—do I wait it out or move forward? Do we pull back our plans or stay on track? Do we trust the stock market, or God? What decision will ultimately prevail? Perhaps more important, do we get excused from the Great Commission during tough times?

WHEN TO INTERVENE WHEN THINGS GO WRONG

My father, Dr. Bill Cooke, was a mainline denominational pastor, and during the late 60s and early 70s he started exploring the Charismatic renewal. As a result, he began teaching on the Holy Spirit, and our church really started growing. There was an explosion of interest in that subject at the time and people started coming from everywhere. But there was one problem: our church had an elder who didn't like it. So the elder began working to undermine my father behind the scenes, and although my dad realized it pretty quickly, he didn't take it seriously. After all, it was just one elder, right?

But this elder was persistent (some might say cunning,) and over the course of a year, he created enough momentum against my dad's teaching that my dad was fired as pastor. My freshman year in college and a thousand miles from home, the first phone call I received from my parents was to tell me that they'd been dismissed from the church.

Since that time, I've seen far too many similar situations. Sometimes it's a theological conflict, other times it's an administrative issue, problem staff member, moral failure, or a challenge to a pastor's leadership style. And in case after case, too many pastors do the same thing as my dad—ignore it until it's too late.

No matter how small, when a crisis starts brewing in a church, when is the best time to intervene?

Now. At that moment. And quickly.

A crisis has a way of escalating. Momentum happens, and before long, people you'd never believe would side with the opposition do exactly that. In many cases, your adversary is strategic, is a good negotiator, and understands how to sway people's thinking.

Don't take anything for granted. As soon as you see, hear, or smell something going south, step in. The earlier you intervene, the easier it will be to change perceptions and correct errors. Plus, the less direct you'll have to be.

KEEPING QUIET IN A CRISIS MAY NOT HELP

Dealing with scandals and problems in the church and ministry world is an even greater challenge in the digital era when information is so readily available. But some techniques from the past still work today.

You may remember the famous Tylenol scare years ago, when some poisoned pills were discovered in a bottle. The president of the company dealt with it immediately, and they spent a fortune on advertising and public service announcements informing the public. Likewise, a winter scheduling disaster by Jet Blue left hundreds of people stuck on planes for hours. The President of the company immediately went on national TV, took the blame, and explained what they were doing to fix it. Mattel did the same with the lead poisoning issue with toys made in China.

Organizations that ignore problems don't last long in a crisis.

The difference between then and now is that in those days they had to spend a fortune on traditional, legacy media. Today, we have social media and can speak to the public for little to no cost.

The strategy that works best is to face up to your problems, talk to the public, and share your strategy for fixing the problem. That has the capacity to win enormous goodwill from the public.

We need to change the way we think about PR in the age of Google. Yes, it was created as a search engine, but it's really about *reputation management*. Numerous organizations have discovered the disastrous side of this equation when they did a search of their company or CEO, only to find negative stories from the past rise to the top. That old DUI you thought everyone had forgotten, the accusation of sexual impropriety, or the nasty e-mail exchange with an ex-employee all find a way to flow into Google's river of information. Religious organizations, companies, and individuals all need to be aware. What can you do?

First—keep the junk to a minimum by living a transparent life. Straighten up, so there isn't any negative information to get out there.

Second—in spite of being transparent, if you've accomplished anything in life, you've probably generated a few critics. So make sure the good stuff gets out. Positive stories need to tell the reality of your organization. The more supportive stories that get out there, the better the chance of the good stuff rising to the top in a search.

Last—use the bloggers and social media influencers. If you have employees, friends, vendors, or supporters who blog, or influential social media users, encourage them to write positive posts and stories about the organization. The more websites and blogs that link to stories about you or the more your social posts are reposted, shared, or commented on—once again—the good stuff rises.

LESSONS FROM JACK GRAHAM ON HANDLING A CRISIS

Whenever I think of "leadership" I think of Jack Graham, pastor of Prestonwood Church in Dallas, Texas. While I've had the incredible opportunity to work with Jack and his PowerPoint media ministry team for many years, when it comes to leadership, there's one memory of Jack that I will never forget.

Many years ago, there was a crisis at the church. It involved a new staff member, and it was serious. So serious, that a press conference had to be called, and the local police were conducting an investigation. The issue was the staff member's problem and had nothing to do with the church, but the church was obviously pulled into the news reports.

When it happened, Jack was speaking at a conference in Israel, and after being notified, he immediately took the first flight back home from Tel Aviv. I was asked to come help Jack and his leadership team craft a strategy for responding. I flew in from Los Angeles and landed a few hours before Jack arrived from overseas. Once he arrived at DFW Airport, he immediately drove to the church—no shower or change of clothes. And when he arrived the press was all assembled.

But before he spoke to the press, he first spoke to the entire church staff—and this moment is what I'll never forget. The staff had been waiting—obviously nervous and unsure of what would happen next. After all, the press was outside ready to pounce. But when Jack walked into the room, you could actually see and hear a sigh of relief from everyone on the team. It was palpable and it was significant. It was as if those employees all felt: "OK. Now Jack's here. Everything is going to be all right."

I will never forget that moment.

As I looked at the response from those employees, I thought, I want to be that kind of leader. I want to inspire such confidence in my team that they feel that as long as I'm there, everything will work out. Jack had led that church through challenges before. They had seen him in action, they'd seen his composure, and they trusted his judgment.

And it did work out. We responded in a way that averted a crisis, and Prestonwood continues to make a positive impact in the Dallas area, across the country, and through their PowerPoint media ministry, around the world.

> **Leaders don't have to know everything, but they need to inspire confidence. When that happens, your team has confidence, and that means you can overcome any obstacle in your way.**

Even though Jack's ministry career is an example of remarkable integrity and credibility, one of the most fascinating aspects of his skill as a leader is how he handles a crisis, and I've been fortunate to see that leadership up close and in action. As a result of watching him lead through challenging situations, here are three important lessons I've learned:

1. Have a plan. In today's world you never know what could happen—accidents, money problems, mistakes, sexual impropriety, baseless allegations—anything. You should coach your team regarding who to call, how to handle the press, and who speaks for the organization. Plan it ahead of time so when a crisis happens, you're not caught off guard.

2. Be honest and tell the truth. In the age of Google, you can't hide anymore. Be upfront, welcome the press when necessary or appropriate, and confront it head-on. Hiding only makes it worse. Jack understands the importance of cooperating with law enforcement, and as a result, they're able to move on with community support. In one case, the PowerPoint media team released a video of Jack's response to a particular situation immediately to the press, and as a result it was seen around the world in a matter of hours. Even Jack's friend, Pastor Greg Laurie, traveling in Rome saw it and sent Jack an encouraging e-mail.

3. Understand the power of "Brand Equity." Back when Billy Graham was preaching, his ministry could weather just about any crisis because they'd spent so many years building up integrity and accountability. Jack and Prestonwood are the same way. Because of their integrity, track record, and involvement in the local community, during a crisis, the public is far more willing to understand and cut them slack. You can't pay for the favor that a lifetime of integrity, accountability, and honesty can bring to a situation.

TODAY, EVERYONE IS A PR PERSON

As social media continues to grow, it's worth reminding everyone on your team that today, "public relations" isn't just for the PR Department. Today, everyone is a PR person. Now, anyone has the ability to influence his or her followers, and it's time we realized the responsibility that involves.

We live in a world where a housewife in rural Oklahoma can bring down a major corporation just through the momentum of social media. Everyone today has a megaphone that reaches enormous numbers of people—it just looks like a mobile device.

> That's why you need to remind everyone
> on your team that the messages they send out
> can have an enormous impact—
> for good or bad—when it comes to
> your business, church, or nonprofit.

The simplest inappropriate tweet can create a public relations crisis, and likewise, positive social media messages can turn around a negative story. That's why you need:

1. A strategy for how to use social media effectively.

2. A meeting (or series of meetings) with your leadership and influencers to teach them the importance of what they share via social media.

3. A vision for how social media can impact your business, church, or nonprofit.

And don't get me wrong. Working with professional PR experts is more important than ever, but your team's understanding of the role they play in getting your story out there can also make an incredibly important (and positive) difference. Because of social media, I actually know organizations where a secretary has more public influence than the CEO, a guy on the loading dock has more public influence than his boss, or an intern with more public influence than her supervisor.

Today, because of the power of social media, everyone's a PR person. Social media doesn't care about titles, seniority, or salaries. Find your organization's influencers and get them on the same page.

IN A CLUTTERED, DIGITAL MEDIA WORLD, DO PRESS RELEASES MATTER?

It may be hard to believe that traditional press releases still matter in the world of social media. After all, with thousands of followers sharing your announcement with all of their followers, word can travel pretty fast. But as important as a social media strategy is to your marketing and communication, there's still a vital place for press releases. The strategy surrounding them has adapted to a digital world, so I asked my friend Larry Ross, founder and CEO of A. Larry Ross Communications in Dallas for his insight. Larry is a public relations expert and his successful relationships with A-List clients is amazing.

Here's what Larry shared with me:

Despite the drastic sea of change in the practice of media and public relations as a result of digital technology, the Internet and the way journalists report and the public consumes the news, the press release (also referred to as a media release, news release, or press statement) is not dead. Rather, it remains a valuable tool in an organization or ministry's publicity arsenal and an essential component of any comprehensive public relations strategy, serving to prime the pump on a given story.

Just as a resume is a requisite foundational element for a prospective job applicant, a well-written press release provides initial and essential information about an individual, organization, or initiative. Press releases have been used by PR pros for decades to inform, educate, and motivate news media to cover an organization, event, product launch, or idea.

Candidly, media representatives no longer exclusively rely on PR professionals to send a press release with information, as they can seek it themselves with a quick Google search or scan of social media platforms. But the press release still serves a very valuable purpose of sharing the overarching, ten-thousand-foot overview of key messages related to an organization's mission, product, event, or leadership.

Further, a press release can live on the Internet through an online newsroom, and is permanently searchable in databases so that media (and consumers) can easily find it as they seek out information. There is also an important search engine optimization (SEO) function to consider, particularly as key words trending in searches on related topics are embedded in the headline, exponentially increasing reach and impact.

However, issuing a press release by itself can't carry the day, and any expectations that interview requests will immediately come flooding in after such a distribution are doomed to fail. It must be supported by a comprehensive public relations plan, or at least accompanied by complementary targeted strategies that reinforce the message to assure media attention, such as:

–> Individual pitch e-mails and personal phone calls to draw out the more specific messaging elements that relate to a reporter's audience or to provide new information beyond what is in the release;

–> Op-eds, articles and blog posts supporting the message of the news release and tying it into news flow and culture; and

–> Social media graphics that visually draw out key messages, and more.

Press releases don't have the same function as they used to, but are still an important part of getting your message out.

THE SECRET TO STOPPING UNWANTED SPECULATION AND RUMOR

Whenever a crisis happens at an organization, rumors begin. We shouldn't be surprised because human beings are wired for curiosity. We want to know what happened, what's going on, and what's next. Channeled in the right direction, curiosity creates inventions, cures disease, and births great art. But channeled in the wrong direction, curiosity can destroy reputations, throw organizations into chaos, and undermine the common good. But there's one way to stop unwanted speculation and rumor in its tracks:

Transparency.

When a crisis happens, curiosity follows. People are going to wonder. Even the most loyal to the cause ask questions. When those questions surface, some in leadership ignore it, while others criticize those asking the questions. But that only causes the problem to fester and grow out of control.

Let me offer a better way:
Without going into lurid detail, just tell the truth.

After Jesus' death and resurrection—and eventual ascension into heaven—the first thing Peter did was to explain to the disciples and friends what happened to Judas. In Acts chapter 1, Peter showed them carefully it was all a fulfillment of scripture. But he didn't stop there. He reminded them that Judas was the man who guided those who arrested Jesus. Then he told them he had "Acquired a field with the reward of his wickedness" and then explained (in detail) how he committed suicide.

He didn't mince words, or call it a personal failure or unspecified sin. Peter told the truth.

But he also didn't go into the gory details.

While the crisis is under investigation, be sensitive, because revealing unfounded or unproven information can permanently destroy reputations. But even then, don't cover up what's happening. And then when investigation ultimately reveals the truth—share it.

When leaders and their organizations are transparent, there's no place left for rumor.

By getting in front of the crisis with the truth, you not only squash the questions, you give people hope that you're moving forward, and there's no reason to fear.

CAN YOU AVOID A FULL-BLOWN CRISIS?

While it's impossible to completely avoid a crisis—especially in larger organizations with many employees—there are ways you can certainly mitigate a PR disaster. It's important to know that it's not about rules—because you can't always enforce rules. Integrity has to be a part of the organization's culture. Nothing's foolproof, but here's a few ideas I follow that might help your organization avoid problems in the future:

1. Build glass offices. Not entirely of course, but when our team remodeled our office building, we installed glass doors in every room. We also added big windows as well. Keep things out in the open in your office design, because if there's nowhere to hide, less hanky-panky can happen.

I suggested this to a ministry leader recently and his response was, "If they really want to have an affair, they'll just do it elsewhere." But in my long experience, the vast majority of moral issues start in the office. Working late, in the intensity of a challenging project, too much casual familiarity—all happen at the office behind closed doors, and if you can keep it from happening there, chances are it won't happen at all.

If you're a leader, the cost of switching your office doors isn't nearly as much as the cost of making the mistake of a lifetime. Obviously there are many reasons for infidelity. But until we solve everything else, my advice is to install glass doors. Make everything in your office public. You'll be glad you did.

2. As a pastor or ministry leader, avoid travelling with someone of the opposite sex unless there's at least one additional employee with you. If you have to travel with a member of the opposite sex that's not your spouse, my recommendation is to *always* bring your spouse or another employee along as well.

3. Have multiple filters for handling finances. When I purchase anything, or return from a trip with travel expenses or receipts, that money or documentation goes from me to my assistant, then to our financial manager, then finally to our CPA. At any stage, they all have the authority to question anything—even though I own the company.

4. No private e-mails. Don't put anything in an e-mail that you wouldn't want printed in the newspaper. Once you hit "send"—you have no idea where that e-mail will end up. A recipient who's your friend today might not be a friend next month. The number of pastors, ministry leaders, or executives that have been fired over e-mails would amaze you. Multiple people in our office have access to my e-mail and social media accounts which seriously cuts my chances of doing anything inappropriate.

5. Web filters for pornography. Particularly if you're a large church or organization, consider investing in web filtering software. Pornography has become so ubiquitous and easily available; it's just not worth the chance.

6. What about the recommendation to meet with members of the opposite sex in public places or with other people in the room? This is the old Billy Graham rule, and some leaders have been criticized recently for following it. I understand that it could limit a woman's time with a male supervisor or leader and potentially hold back her career. But it's ultimately an individual question, and each of us have to answer it for ourselves.

WHAT TO DO WHEN YOU RECEIVE UNWANTED SEXUAL OR PROVOCATIVE MESSAGES FROM AN ADMIRER

You don't have to be a leader for long before you start receiving unwanted e-mails, text messages, or phone calls from various "admirers." While some may be innocent or misunderstood, it's difficult to tell at the start, and for the sake of your reputation and integrity, I recommend you take no chances. I've seen leaders who have stepped down or been fired because of this issue, so please take it seriously. Remember that e-mail isn't private. In a legal case, a police investigation or a simple hack, and your emails, text messages, social media, and phone records can become public in an instant.

If you start receiving suggestive photos, intimate messages, or find that someone of either sex is reaching out to you inappropriately or without your invitation, here's what I recommend:

1. Don't respond. Just a response to unwanted messages could be taken as a sign that you welcomed the messages, or that you were involved. Plus, for trolls or someone obsessed with you, any response at all is an encouragement.

2. Alert your closest associates. Share the message with your assistant, close associate, spouse, and even your attorney. Making it public early shows that the messages were unwanted. I received this kind of e-mail a few years ago from a woman who heard me speak at a conference overseas. When I received her e-mail I not only shared it with my wife, our female assistant, and a producer in our company—I had my assistant respond. Once the female "admirer" knew that my female assistant was reading my e-mail, we never heard from her again.

3. If it's persistent, you should block them. If that doesn't work, don't hesitate to block the e-mail address, phone number, or social media accounts. In most cases, that's all it takes to stop unwanted communication. But if that doesn't stop them, then get a new e-mail address or mobile number. Integrity is worth the inconvenience.

4. In some cases, you may want to give your assistant access to your e-mail account. I work with a number of pastors and leaders who do this, and I do it myself. That's a pretty good accountability method, because you can't be fooling around when others have access to your e-mail.

5. If you deem it serious enough (sexually explicit photos, threats, provocative messages, etc.) then by all means get your attorney's advice. What seems simple today can easily escalate into a legal situation tomorrow.

6. Finally—in those serious cases, also get advice from a trusted media and communications expert. There are some great attorneys out there whose goal is to win your case or protect you legally—and save your reputation. But saving your reputation isn't always a priority in the courtroom. In my work with pastors and leaders in this area, there have been cases where my clients followed good legal advice, but years later, because the legal decision became a public document, it hurt them in the press. Beyond an attorney's legal strategy, a trusted media counselor will help advise you on how the public, press, congregation, or donors will respond. Getting good legal and communication counsel together now can help deflect miscommunication, bad assumptions, and an unfriendly reporter's agenda in the future.

Sexual harassment and abuse is inexcusable, and it's good that bad leaders are being forced to step down. But at the same time, there are good men and women who have simply not responded well when a potentially damaging situation was instigated by others. In a digital world, it's easier than ever for an unwanted admirer or troll to contact you by e-mail, phone, texting, or social media. The key is to never put yourself in a situation where things could be interpreted incorrectly, and if you do, take immediate steps to correct it.

HOW TO REACT WHEN A PASTOR OR MINISTRY LEADER EXPERIENCES A MORAL FAILURE

Pastors experience moral failings, staff members embezzle money, leaders turn out to be pedophiles, serial adulterers, incompetent, the list goes on and on. Every situation is different, and the goals include healing the victim, responding to the leader according to biblical principles, and keeping the church healthy. Seeking God is essential, but along with that process, there are some immediate practical choices that have to be made. If you're a church leader, elder, board member, or know someone who is, this is a priority list you should share and keep handy just in case a crisis happens in your church:

1. **Prepare for a crisis ahead of time.** Research shows that organizations that have a crisis plan recover much more quickly (and with less cost) than those who don't. And don't think a crisis can't happen to you. In today's complex, digital world, the chances your church or ministry will have problems has only increased. Pray, hope for the best, but always have a plan if something goes wrong.

2. **Get an attorney's advice immediately.** There are numerous legal issues surrounding these types of failings, and you don't want to put the church at risk. Pastors have been arrested because they didn't respond to a crisis according to local laws. That's why a qualified attorney should be your first call.

3. **Know your liability insurance policy.** In many cases, lawsuits happen, and a good insurance policy can literally save the church. It's one thing for a leader to fail, but quite another for him or her to take the entire church down in the process. Talk to your insurance agent as well as your attorney, and make sure you're covered for these types of situations.

4. **When a crisis happens, don't cover it up.** Leaks happen, and they will happen to you. In the digital era we live in, it's not just our theology or moral

principles at issue, it's about telling the story and getting the facts straight. Otherwise, in our digital culture things can spin out of control pretty quickly and rumors and lies will mount up. You're living in a dream world if you believe you can hide it or keep a lid on it for long.

5. Be honest. You don't have to reveal everything about the situation, but whatever you do, don't make anything up or hide anything. Don't obscure, embellish, or deflect. It will always come back to haunt you. That doesn't mean you blurt out everything you know, but it does mean whatever you say must be true—according to what you know at the time.

Even when you think you're trying to help, lies will be found out. The worst situation is to be forced to change your story as new information is revealed. Be honest from the beginning.

6. If possible, break the news to your church family first. This is indeed a family, and they need to be told in person. Don't e-mail the news, tell it to them live. Sometimes that's difficult if the problem happens early in the week, because it's tough to keep a lid on it until the weekend services. But if possible, and especially if the news comes to light toward the end of the week, I'm an advocate of sharing the truth with the congregation first. They deserve to hear the real story, not rumors, gossip, or through the local news.

7. Then go public and tell the story. Through an official statement, press release, or local news story, I encourage the church to tell the story of what happened. You don't need to go into inappropriate detail, but at some level, the story needs to be told. If you don't, the press will report anything they can find including rumors, second-hand gossip, and speculation. If you don't tell your side of what happened, the other side's story will remain on the record forever.

8. Seek counseling, healing, and restoration for all parties. You should be impartial when it comes to helping everyone heal. And whatever you do, in the case of church or ministry leader's moral failure, never criticize or demean the other party involved. Particularly at this early date, no one knows everything about the situation, so never come across as harsh or unfeeling towards anyone. You need to express genuine sympathy, assure the public that you're arranging counseling, and are working to resolve the issue. In the midst of the initial chaos, dealing with the spiritual and psychological issues are paramount.

9. If the allegations are true, pull the pastor or leader's content from your website, print materials, church bookstore, and everywhere else. After stepping down from leadership because of a failing, his or her presence in these and other places will only confuse the situation. Make a clean break and make it quickly. Teaching resources, downloads, podcasts, videos, broadcast radio or TV programming, social media platforms, books, and more should all be taken down or closed. If you don't, critics will use online photos and videos to make fun of the situation and it can get ugly.

10. Get communications advice from a professional. Activate a crisis team. Get them together, go over the situation and implement your strategy. (You've already developed a crisis strategy just in case, right?). Good attorneys can help with the legal issues, but an experienced crisis communication and media professional can help you know what to say, how to say it, and when to say it. Writing official statements and press releases can be tricky. Setting up a press conference can backfire. Talk to someone who has been there and can help you plan. The cost will not only save an enormous amount down the road but it can save the church's reputation.

11. Start moving the church forward immediately. Members of your congregation will grieve, but for the church to survive, you need to keep moving forward. Tell your leaders, teachers, and small groups not to dwell on the failing, but talk about the future. Keep programs intact. Plan new events. Refocus the congregation from the failing in the past, to the possibilities of the future. At the same time, keep the press informed when necessary, work on counseling for everyone involved, and make the necessary changes in the organization's leadership structure.

The more you hide, the more people will assume you're not telling the whole truth.

Be ready for critics of all kinds, because even some Christians inexperienced in these matters will criticize a crisis plan as not being spiritual, or trying to manipulate the truth. But it's not about manipulation, it's about being honest. It's not about contriving a story, it's about revealing the truth. However—it needs to be handled in an appropriate way so more lives aren't damaged, and the church doesn't suffer even more.

While some may think a strategy like this is harsh or insensitive, the scrutiny can be white hot, and without the right response, negative press coverage and word of mouth can destroy an otherwise great church, ministry, or nonprofit.

And that's the primary point here. You don't want a great work undermined or destroyed because of the inappropriate actions of one person. Don't act out of fear, anger, or retribution, but act, and act now.

God is a good God. Restoration and healing can happen. But taking the right steps from the beginning will make a big difference. God forbid anything like this will ever happen to your church or ministry, but just in case, share this with your leadership team so they'll know what to do if and when that time comes.

BE SURE YOU'RE RESPONDING TO THE RIGHT AUDIENCE DURING A PR CRISIS

As you've seen, there are many challenges to confront during a public relations crisis. Perhaps one of the most misunderstood is understanding your audience. Certainly it's important to respond as the spiritual leader that you are. However, it's important to respond in the right way at the right time; otherwise, it undermines the trust of your supporters.

For instance, if you're a religious organization facing allegations of financial improprieties, then just a "spiritual" answer isn't appropriate. Trying to assure supporters that God will deliver you, or that Satan won't destroy the ministry isn't what the congregation, partners, or donors are looking for.

They're looking for professional assurances that financial safeguards are in place, and integrity is your priority.

If it's a financial crisis, don't just respond like a pastor or evangelist. Respond like a professional.

Whatever the problem, respond to that issue from the perspective of that issue.

DOES HAVING A SPOKESPERSON HELP?

One idea that may seem counterintuitive is that often, rather than having the leader speak for the organization, sometimes it's more effective to have someone else. You've seen examples with the White House, who has a press spokesperson holding press conferences in lieu of the president. Many corporations do the same thing.

The purpose is to have an information layer between the leader and the media. Whatever the size of your church, nonprofit, or business, you may need a spokesperson. Even if you're involved in positive work like assisting after natural disasters you'll encounter the media on many levels, so it's always good to put your best foot forward. What makes a good spokesperson?

1. They know how to deal with the outside media. Today, media interviews can be tough, and it's not unusual for some media professionals to be deceptive in pursuit of a better story. Which means an inexperienced spokesperson can be a disaster. If you don't have anyone with media experience, consider media training, which can make a dramatic difference in his or her ability to perform well at a press conference or media interview.

2. They should be articulate and professional looking. You want them to represent you in a crisis, so they need to speak well, use good grammar, and be credible. In a crisis, perceptions matter.

3. They need to know your organization. There's nothing worse than a spokesperson who doesn't have answers—especially if they don't know your organization and its position, capabilities, or policies. If they're not an in-house employee, take the time to teach them about your organization. If they don't have answers, they'll lose credibility quickly.

4. They need to express trust. If the media believes they aren't telling the truth, or holding back for any reason, things won't go well. They need to express confidence and credibility or the media will look elsewhere for answers.

5. They need to be ready quickly. In a crisis or disaster, an enormous amount happens in the first twenty-four to forty-eight hours. That's when you have the media's attention, it's when the most fundraising happens after a disaster (people are impulse givers), and when most people are watching. Lose that window, and you lose your voice.

6. They are calm. During a crisis, everything hits the fan. Of all people, your media spokesperson needs to be calm, collected, and professional. If they lose their cool, you lose the trust of everyone. No matter how tense or hostile things get, you need a point person who looks in control.

Start looking for the right spokesperson for your organization. It can be the CEO, board member, a communication director, or outside consultant. Whoever it is, help them represent you as well as possible to the media. The value of an effective spokesperson can't be calculated.

HOW TO HANDLE INTERVIEWS WITH SECULAR REPORTERS

One of the biggest questions I hear from pastors and media leaders is whether or not they should agree to an interview with the secular media. Sometimes it's about something positive, like launching a new or innovative ministry outreach, but more often, it's about something negative.

In today's world, where journalism seems to have lost its compass, and it's more like marketing than actual reporting, we all wonder how journalists look at the world. There are plenty of misconceptions about reporters, but here are some insights worth noting before you accept your next interview:

Am I obligated to respond to media requests? Absolutely not. Never feel like you're being backed into a corner. Sometimes it's important to respond to a crisis or other issue, and there are plenty of times it can help. But there's no rule that you have to talk to any reporter at any time they request an interview. That's your decision.

Are reporters out to get you? Maybe a few, but in most cases no. They're not necessarily interested in making you look bad, but they are out for a story, and if making you look bad is the price to pay, then many are willing to let that happen.

Years ago a major ministry leader was ambushed on a national news program. He was lured in with the hook that the reporter had heard he was being considered as the next Billy Graham. That ego boost was hard to turn down, but during the interview, the reporter turned the tables and showed him evidence of financial wrongdoing at his ministry.

It was a national news program so his entire ministry crashed almost overnight. The lesson? Put your ego aside and do some homework. As I said before, you're under no obligation to meet with the press, so simply be careful.

Do reporters skillfully edit interviews to say what they want? (Regardless of what was actually said.) It doesn't happen often, but it does happen. Plus, the pressure to edit down a full length interview into the short space of a news report can make for some very inaccurate statements and biased perceptions. Some ministry leaders will bring their own camera to an interview and record the entire session themselves just to have proof of what was actually discussed. I don't know if that's always necessary, but it does put the reporter on notice that you'll have a record of the actual conversation.

Does the media have an agenda? Sadly yes. As we've seen in this polarized culture, different media organizations have a bias, so it's important to know who's doing the interview.

What happens if the reporter just lets me talk? That usually ends up being a disaster. This is a very strange thing, but very often in an interview the reporter will just stop talking. The interviewee feels that somehow he or she should say something to fill the silence, so they just start rambling.

And that is where you get killed. Invariably, the interviewee will blurt out something in that space that will be their undoing. I don't fully understand it, but it happens far more often than you'd think. For the record, it's a technique police interrogators use as well. The lesson? If the reporter stops asking questions, then you stop answering.

Does the media look for controversy? Absolutely. Controversy gets viewers and attention. Controversy sells. Never do an interview without realizing that fact.

Now—are you ready when a reporter comes calling?

SIX STEPS TO GREAT PUBLICITY

I've spent a great deal of time in this chapter focusing on the negative, so let's finish on a positive note. Everyone today is a PR person, but from time to time you may get a book published, produce a movie, lead a major event, or do something else significant and have the opportunity to work with a public relations firm or publicist. Their job is to attract attention to your outreach, book, film, movement, business—whatever. But hiring a publicist isn't a magic button. Perhaps in the old days of legacy media, you hired a publicity expert and then sat back and collected big paychecks based on book sales.

But not today. To work successfully with a PR expert or publicist, here's some important keys:

1. It's a partnership, not a one-man show. They need your help, so don't sign the contract and then check out. The PR firm or publicist needs your input on press releases, pitch information, and more. Show up, make yourself available, and you'll be far more successful.

2. Help create content. During my last few book releases, I worked with a publicity firm that asked me to write some opinion pieces based on current issues I discussed in my books. They were able to get those columns published in some amazing places like *WIRED* magazine, *Fast Company, Forbes,* and more. But here's the key: I had to write them. If you can write six-hundred-word op-ed pieces based on your book, film, business idea, or cause, it will make a remarkable difference in helping you get the story out there.

3. **Bring your assets to the table.** Do you lead a large company? Have a successful blog? Do a radio program? Pastor a large church? The best place to start a publicity campaign is with people who already know and like you. Give your publicity consultant a running start by helping them reach the low hanging fruit of your friends, fans, church members, or followers.

4. **It will take time.** The publicist's contacts have to be pitched, they need to look over your book or film, and they need to schedule it into their media run. Don't expect miracles in the first month. Give them time to launch your campaign and you'll see much more significant benefits. Because of that, you need to be engaging a publicity firm at least a month or two before the book or project release date.

5. **Don't take it personally.** I've been turned down by plenty of major media outlets, but I don't let that get me down. I also don't blame it on my PR person. They got me there, and it was the news director, editor, or station manager who said no. It's not about you, it's about what that particular news program needs to advance its agenda. If your story doesn't fit, then fine. Move on.

6. **Finally, be open to interviews at weird times or for small platforms.** I've been up at 3 a.m. my time to do a network TV interview for the 6 a.m. news on the East Coast. I've done phone interviews long after midnight with a radio station in Perth, Australia. I've been interviewed by magazines I've never heard of, unfamiliar podcasts, and obscure small college radio stations. But guess what? You never know who's listening. Some of my best speaking engagements or consulting projects came because of someone who was listening to a small radio station or reading a local newspaper.

I randomly had breakfast with the vice president of a major nonprofit organization while on a trip to India. We were staying at the same hotel. When I introduced myself, he told me as he was leaving his house for the airport, his wife gave him a magazine with my interview in it and told him to read it on the plane. What were the odds that we'd meet halfway around the world? Now he wants me to speak at their annual conference, and it would have never happened without that magazine interview.

Be open to all the possibilities, because you never know where publicity will lead.

KEY PRINCIPLES TO CONSIDER ABOUT HANDLING A CRISIS:

1. **It's not *if* you'll have a crisis, it's *when*.** The key is to be ready and develop a plan long before anything happens.

2. **In today's social media world, chances are far greater that an employee will say something inappropriate.** Spend time with your team—especially leaders identified with your church or organization. Help them understand that what they say on social media—even on their personal platforms—can reflect in a positive or negative way on the church or ministry.

3. **In the heat of a crisis, don't spend time looking for blame.** Be proactive and get the problem under control. There will be plenty of time later to examine what went wrong.

4. **Always seek the advice of two key people in a crisis:** An *attorney* for the legal aspects of the issue, and a *public relations or communication professional* for advice on how to respond.

5. **A great reputation can't save you from a crisis, but it's always the place to start.** Never take chances with your reputation, because your critics will have a tougher time when they have less to criticize.

6. **Sometimes it's better not to respond.** Particularly when it comes to criticism on social media. Consider the source, think about your options, and get advice from an expert before you step into the firing line.

AFTERWORD

"It has always been my ambition to preach the gospel where Christ was not known."
—The Apostle Paul in Romans 15:20

During the COVID-19 crisis in 2020 the Church was faced with a choice: *go online or go out of business.* When the shutdown was mandated, pastors and church leaders who had previously been skeptical about media were suddenly willing to take a chance. I'd been preaching the digital message for decades, but when options became limited, even the skeptics started to pay attention. It reminded me of the quote by Samuel Johnson from the year 1777: *"Depend upon it, sir, when a man knows he is to be hanged in a fortnight, it concentrates his mind wonderfully."*

As pastors and church leaders responded, surprising things happened around the world. Over and over churches reported their live stream audience was three to four times the size of any crowd who had ever attended a worship service. More people were accepting Christ than ever, and in cases where giving was down, it wasn't because of the service being live streamed as much as the vast number of people who were suddenly out of work.

During that time I wrote a blog post about what pastors should be considering as we emerge from the crisis, and one pastor who leads a congregation of nine hundred members texted me to say:

When this crisis started we only had 80 YouTube subscribers; now we have 23,000. A single sermon of mine has been viewed by almost 1.5 million people. In the last weeks we have had about 95,000 views of our services. We are actually reaching far more people than we have done in years. I wish I felt bad saying this but I don't—I'm really not in a hurry to get back into the building. . . .

While we all value worship services in our church buildings, for pastors, leaders, and communication teams at churches around the globe, the experience of online church was an eye-opening moment. During the first four weeks of the shutdown in 2020, I taught thousands of pastors and church communication leaders through my blog, Zoom lectures, webinars, and online classes.

This book was published during the transition out of that shutdown, and the future only knows if church leaders will continue embracing their online worship experience as intentionally once people are back in the church. My hope is that they will.

Whatever the size of your church, your experience, and the level of your communication team, there has never been a time in the history of the world when so many tools have been available to share your message with so many people.

Before His ascension, Jesus gave His followers one last great command: *"All authority in heaven and on earth has been given to me. Therefore go and make disciples of all nations, baptizing them in the name of the Father and of the Son and of the Holy Spirit, and teaching them to obey everything I have commanded you. And surely I am with you always, to the very end of the age."*

When Jesus challenged the disciples with The Great Commission in Matthew 28:18-20, the world was a smaller place, and yet the goal must have seemed impossible. In that period, along with preaching, New Testament writers like the Apostle Paul used *letters*—the media platform of the time to build the Church. The early Church faced persecution, heretics—and yes, plague—but those letters still got the job done.

And the year 2020 proved that a modern day plague like COVID-19 was no match for the *digital tools* available to the Church today. Those tools not only overcame a global shutdown, but they continue to allow us to speak to a worldwide audience. Online, previously little-known churches, ministries, and their leaders can now influence millions.

The need to share our message never changes,
but *how* we share it does. This is the moment to
embrace the digital world. You don't have to be famous,
you just need to have something to say that matters,
and nothing matters more than the gospel.

ADDITIONAL RESOURCES

Find More Resources for Pastors and Leaders at:
PhilCooke.com

Cooke Media Group:
CookeMediaGroup.com

The Influence Lab:
InfluenceLab.com

Books by Phil Cooke:
*The Way Back: How Christians Blew Our Credibility and How We
Get It Back* (co-written with Jonathan Bock)—Hachette Book Group
*Unique: Telling Your Story in the Age of Brands
and Social Media*—Baker Books
One Big Thing: Discovering What You Were Born to Do—
Thomas Nelson Publishers
Unique: The Ultimate Planner for Creative Professionals—
Broadstreet Publishing
*The Last TV Evangelist: Why the Next Generation Couldn't Care Less
About Religious Media and Why It Matters*—Conversant Media Group
Phil Cooke on Creativity—E-book available on Amazon.com
Medio Creativo Cristiano—Secretos De Exito Del Ministerio De Medios—
E-book available on Amazon.com
Jolt! Get the Jump on a World That's Constantly Changing—
Thomas Nelson Publishers

Connect with Phil:
Phil's blog: PhilCooke.com
Facebook: @philcookepage
Twitter: @philcooke
Instagram: @philcooke

ABOUT THE AUTHOR

Phil Cooke has produced TV and film programming or lectured in nearly one hundred countries around the world, and in the process, been shot at, survived two military coups, fallen out of a helicopter, and in Africa, been threatened with prison. And during that time—through his company Cooke Media Group in Los Angeles, California—he's helped some of the largest Christian and nonprofit organizations in the world use media to tell their story in a changing, disrupted culture.

Phil was executive producer of *Let Hope Rise—the Hillsong Movie* released to theaters nationwide, and producer of *The Insanity of God,* a feature documentary that premiered nationally as a Fathom Event. According to former CNN journalist Paula Zahn, Phil is rare—"the only working producer in Hollywood with a Ph.D. in Theology." He's appeared on NBC, MSNBC, CNBC, CNN, Fox News, and his work has been profiled in *The New York Times*, the *Los Angeles Times*, and the *Wall Street Journal.*

He has lectured at universities like Yale, University of California at Berkeley, UCLA, and is currently a visiting professor at Oral Roberts University in Tulsa, Oklahoma. In addition to writing his blog at philcooke.com, he's contributed to The Huffington Post, *Fast Company,* Forbes.com, Wired.com, and FoxNews.com. Phil is on advisory boards for The Salvation Army, the Hollywood Prayer Network, and *Image Journal.* He has been a longtime member of the Academy of Television Arts and Sciences and The Producers Guild of America in Hollywood.